TIGER BY THE TAIL

TIGER BY THE TAIL

99 SECRETS TO TAME AND MASTER YOUR BUSINESS

MARTY PARK

LIONCREST
PUBLISHING

TIGER BY THE TAIL

99 Secrets to Tame and Master Your Business

ISBN   978-1-5445-0528-2 *Hardcover*
       978-1-5445-0529-9 *Paperback*
       978-1-5445-0530-5 *Ebook*

To my clients, who have realized that the "fun" really begins
after you start the business. You have all the skills, talents,
and abilities necessary to build incredible organizations.

To my business mentors, Dad, and HoHo, thank you for
twenty-five years of business guidance and advice.

To my wife, Lisa, for your support and belief that
I have a voice and knowledge to share.

CONTENTS

INTRODUCTION

TAMING THE TIGER

The first time I grabbed the tiger by the tail, I wasn't ready. A friend and I decided to leave university and partner in business. We figured that starting a software company was the fast track to success. Everyone knew that creating a company like Microsoft was the only way to go, and we firmly believed that we'd strike it rich and retire in about six months. How tough could it be?

We had what many entrepreneurs and first-time business owners have—what I call, "blissful ignorance." If we had known, or had the slightest idea what we were in for, we might not have attempted it. I would have stayed in school, gotten a degree, and changed the course of my life.

Instead, I have experienced the unforeseeable highs and

lows that can only come from being an entrepreneur and business operator. I have signed seven-figure contracts and I've feared the bank foreclosing on my loans. I have built physical businesses from the ground up, from concept, design, and construction to opening. I have also been so broke that I worried about having enough money to put gas in my car just to get to work.

I have moved in and out of multiple industries based on what seemed interesting to me at the time. No science to it, just intuition. Many will suggest that this isn't the best approach to choosing companies or industries, but I have always moved toward things based on instinct first, and business evaluation second. I believe that both are required to make a venture work.

Since my first software company, I have operated thirteen other companies in six different industries, giving me a depth of experience obtained by few entrepreneurs. Along the way, I've developed strategies to grab hold of the tiger of business, tame it, and ride it to the finish line.

MORE THAN A MARATHON

Most books discuss the start-up phase of a business, but what many people don't realize is that deciding to begin a business is the easy part. Early on, a start-up is primarily a checklist of actions and steps before beginning operations. Picking a name, designing a logo, securing a lease, ordering inventory, and finding a supplier are all relatively easy. It takes months to get it all done, but like training for a marathon, it's just a lead-up to the main event. It may be challenging and strenuous, but it's nothing compared to what the actual race will be like with competition on the field.

The fact is that business is far more than a marathon. Compared to running a business, a marathon is more like a sprint, just a quick moment in time. Entrepreneurship is a years-long, ongoing process of growth, challenge, and development. Every day is game day. If it were only three to six hours long, like an average marathon race, people would be signing up and winning at business all the time. Unlike a race with a finish line, business ownership is a nonstop endeavor, demanding peak performance at all times. It wears many people down.

Entrepreneurship only really starts when you sell something, which is the first step in the race. Until you actually make a sale, all the actions you are taking are simply preparation. You may be hiring, producing, and systemizing operations, but nothing matters until you sell something. Only sales will justify your efforts, which is why I am a huge sales advocate. It is the critical driver of every company, whether you are selling goods or services. Sales is when the rubber hits the road. It's where all the challenges, variables, and situations unique to your business, and common to all businesses, finally begin.

Yes, each type of business is unique, yet all are remarkably the same. I have worked with companies and owners worldwide, and I've seen that everyone tends to think that their location, industry, or product makes them totally different. It doesn't. Every business is trying to sell or market something, administer it, finance it, staff it, or produce it. There are universal problems that arise requiring universal solutions. So, if you're wondering whether this book will address your business and your unique circumstances, you can rest assured that it will. The universal nature of business is indisputable.

THE IMPORTANCE OF MINDSET

Above all, I emphasize mindset, because the owner's mindset is the strongest determining factor for the success of any company. It is where ideas are initially hatched and evaluated. The owner's mind is central for determining how a business runs day-to-day. The owner provides inspiration and direction for all decision-making. A company's business operations are a direct reflection of the owner and their thought process. The owner's mindset is the foundation for the success or failure of the business.

However, there comes a time when every entrepreneur

and business owner can lose sight of their capabilities. That's where this book comes in. My hope and objective is that in reading this book, you are inspired to keep going and hold fast to your entrepreneurial dream. On these pages I provide actionable, nonacademic solutions to the challenges and business problems facing every entrepreneur. Here you will find the strategies and tactics that will make winning the race of business ownership easier.

Running a company is the most challenging choice someone can make. It's a fast-moving game where the players change position and the field shifts every day, but one where you can change the rules and innovate to create a new game. If you are already operating a company, then you know the daunting challenge you have chosen. I believe that entrepreneurship is the most rewarding career choice a person can make. Nothing drives your learning and development like running a business. Nothing makes you reflect more on "you" than the struggles of business ownership and operation.

One of my favorite moments as a business coach was with a former client who went from operating a successful furniture business to deciding she was going to launch a fashion store. She said it had finally occurred to her that she was no longer just a furniture business owner, but a cross-industry entrepreneur. She had come to understand, in mind and heart, that she had the know-how and skills to start any company she wanted, and make it a success.

HOW TO USE THIS BOOK

I wish you this kind of personal confidence and transformation to expand your belief in yourself as a visionary entrepreneur without limits. What follows are 99 Secrets that will help you realize your dreams with the business you are considering, the one you are operating, and the ones you'll create in the future.

Most businesses have areas that are running great, and other areas that struggle. What makes it more complicated is that those areas change constantly; it can seem like your team is working well, then suddenly a couple of key employees give notice and HR is in a tailspin! Your cash flow is smooth, then the summer months hit, and suddenly you need more clients and cash to stay afloat.

This book is a resource for both practical advice and real-life business stories. I encourage you to read it from cover to cover, over and over. Mark the pages, make notes, use the links, and go to the website for tools, templates, and instructions to put these secrets into action in your company.

www.tigerbythetailbook.com

For easy reference, the 99 Secrets are grouped into sections of business functions, and other sections focused on you, the owner. This structure allows you to concentrate on issues and solutions as you need them. You can flip to a section to review ideas, or you can open to any page to discover an idea that applies to you now, or perhaps in six months when you need it.

Everything you need to be a great entrepreneur and business owner today resides inside you, right now. This book will help you bring those capacities to the surface so you can put them to work.

Are you ready for the first secret to tame the tiger and master your business?

PART ONE

YOUR MINDSET IS 95 PERCENT OF THE BATTLE

The things you say to yourself when running a company, the thoughts you have and the beliefs you hold to be true are absolutely critical. They guide the way you make decisions and the actions you take in your business every day. This is your mindset. It's your way of thinking and believing. Mindset is your intention. It's what makes you tick.

Your mindset accounts for 95 percent of your long-term success as an entrepreneur. It's therefore important to be honest about your mindset because it will guide your playbook long before anything happens in your business operationally. Limitations in your mindset will constrain you before any limits in your market, your budget, or your ability.

Why don't most business owners create ubersuccessful companies that are market leaders? It's because they are unable to see their organization becoming that successful. The business you create follows the size, scope, and clarity of your mental picture. The ultimate success of your business requires the highest level of belief in yourself and your intention building toward your goal.

Limitation and scarcity need to be identified within yourself and kept in check to create your business masterpiece. Don't let those in the market, in your family, or in your firm restrict what you see as opportunities to create. It's vital to make your power to think, innovate, and produce, stronger than any external limitation. Mastery of your business starts with how you think about it, and how you follow through to create it. Success begins with mindset.

PERSISTENCE, ADAPT, PERSISTENCE

———

Do you want to know what characteristic will help you master and succeed in your company more than any other?

Hands down, no doubt, undeniably, it's the attitude and commitment of persistence.

So often for entrepreneurs, problems and issues come up that don't have textbook solutions. When the recession of 2008–2009 hit companies around the world hard, entrepreneurs didn't know where to turn for answers. Everyone was dealing with an overarching situation of lower sales, financial pressure, and failing markets.

Solutions aren't always obvious. It can be like diagnosing a patient with multiple symptoms. Diagnosing a business problem can involve many variables to the equation. When trouble hits, my first piece of advice is to take it easy on yourself. If you don't know the answer immediately to every issue you face, you are just like everyone else. You are in the same struggle as every other entrepreneur and owner. Give yourself a break and don't pressure yourself to come up with an answer straight off.

With a clear frame of mind you can dig in and start looking for solutions. Depending on the particular challenge, it can take days, weeks, or even years of persistence to find the appropriate resolution.

I once had an issue in building a restaurant where my outdoor patio application was not included in the original design and building approvals. When I went back to the city to get an approval, they literally laughed at me. They said there was no way I would ever get an approval. Yet the patio was a key part of our business model; it doubled our seating in the summer months! I was angry and determined to find a way. I just wouldn't take no for an answer.

I spent the next three years using consultants, meeting with community reps, getting letters and signatures, and learning the process at city hall. I met with councilmen, submitted rezoning plans for a whole city block, and applied for my own patio permits. I fought a legal battle with a single neighbor who opposed the patio (and who happened to be a lawyer). I was persistent, very persistent, and at every step I adapted my tactics.

Friends, family, staff, other business owners, city officials, the building developer, consultants, and even my business partner suggested we give up. Many times I also wanted to quit, but I just couldn't. I knew somewhere deep down that there had to be a way. I was prepared to put more effort into success than everyone I faced was prepared to put into defeating me.

Finally, I went to the city council to make my case in front of the highest level of municipal leaders. I had met them repeatedly and even developed a relationship with some.

In the end, my lobbying and efforts paid off—my patio was approved only three-and-a-half years after the restaurant opened! It was absolutely gratifying and had a tremendous impact on our business. I had been through anger, despair, frustration, confusion, hope, and gridlock. I wanted to murder some of the civic workers who were denying me my rights. I saw how government and business do not always mix.

That experience taught me a valuable lesson that applies across the board to business. Persistence in sales, financing, staffing, (and even patios), is the most critical skill you can have. It involves the constant effort to succeed and overcome. Persistence can help you look at a problem from angles that others just can't or won't see. In many parts of business, such as in product development, persistence goes hand in hand with innovation. Innovation, or adaptation, is critical to growth. Combined with innovation, persistence keeps you looking at things differently and finding new angles for solutions. Persistence is the ability to adapt your approach to every problem to find unique solutions. If you do nothing else but persist in your company, you will achieve more success than most people.

TWENTY TIMES THE PROBLEMS

———

Running a company involves twenty times the problems than most people experience in their workday. The insurance clerk dealing with accident paperwork deals with the same issues day in and day out. It's like the movie *Groundhog Day*, every day looks the same. A receiving clerk may complain about a shipment that didn't arrive, and that he had to call the client to tell them their order was going to be late. That's it? That's not a problem, that's a phone call.

The problems on a regular job pale before the problems that face an entrepreneur. If you feel overwhelmed by the number of problems you have on your plate, you are in the sweet spot of entrepreneurship.

The shipping clerk has his problems and the finance manager has her problems, but the entrepreneur gets them all. On any given day, the business owner is dealing with an issue of sale price, inventory shortage, a sick staff person, rent due, a marketing deadline, and operations. Tomorrow it's another set of problems. And it's just Tuesday! When your expertise needs to span every aspect of the business, your issues also span every aspect of the business.

All problems force you to expand your knowledge and skills in all areas NOW! It is seriously challenging, but can also be rewarding as you grow in skills and knowledge. One of the keys is to embrace all of these situations that make you feel ill-equipped, because they force you to learn. It's important to consciously decide to recognize the pace of change and growth required of the entrepreneur, and learn to enjoy it.

Any day that you are struggling with some customer issue, a finance issue, a sales issue, a staff or production issue is a normal day. It takes a great deal of skill and determination (and persistence) to get up each day, knowing the level of headache you will face.

Here are several keys to operating in this environment while still being able to sleep at night:

- Recognize that this is the adventure of running a company. You are doing it right.

- While most people panic about issues, your success will come when you realize that no issue is resulting in the death of people or total calamity. (My slogan is, "Folks, we aren't curing cancer here, so let's relax.")
- Recognize that a problem or issue is external to you. Although the tendency is to internalize a problem and allow it to create festering stress, remind yourself that the issue is outside yourself.
- Look to see where you can not only solve an issue, but start to systemize how you can solve the problem in the future. If it happens more than two or three times, it is likely a system problem. Develop a standard response or process that your whole team can manage.
- Look at who you can pull into the solution; who else in the company should be and can be part of the solution? Too often, owners assume all problems are theirs to fix. As soon as staff can be empowered to solve a problem the way you want, it instantly takes the pressure off you and starts to create a team of problem solvers. (Note: Your staff will take a Band-Aid solution over a good solution about 85 percent of the time. Therefore, make sure that your staff understands the difference between a superficial solution and a real solution).

A very successful entrepreneur I know, Peter Thomas, faced bankruptcy, potentially owing $100 million from a real estate deal gone wrong. Now, that is a problem! He got through that period of his life, and after that, he didn't find any issue as daunting as what he'd already been through. His slogan became, "This will be easy," and he'd say it every time some bump in the road came up. It set the tone for him and the people around him. Finding solutions to challenges became a lot easier. He has been exceptionally successful in business and life. Such a profound change in mindset can reframe problems and set a can-do attitude that fosters appropriate actions and solutions.

YOU MEAN I'M NOT THE ONLY ONE?

———

Let me state this in no uncertain terms: It's not just you. It's not just you worrying. It's not just you struggling. It's not just you awake at night stressing about keeping it together.

A young start-up entrepreneur asked me at a conference, "When do you stop worrying about money?" He said he couldn't sleep, he was always up at night trying to solve his cash problems and reevaluating everything.

I told him that I referred to this as the "2 a.m. Entrepreneur Alarm Clock." Your stress hormones kick in, you're wide awake, you can't let go of your issues, and you feel overwhelmed. You can't sleep and you wrestle with just getting out of bed in the morning to start your day.

I told him there was good news and bad news:

The bad news is that you never stop worrying about cash and cash flow.

The good news is that your threshold for worrying changes.

Right now he's worried about $500. In the coming years, it will take a $5,000 issue to keep him up at night. Then, as his company grows, he'll find himself sleeping soundly until he has a $10,000 issue. Eventually that will grow to $100,000 to make him sweat.

As your experience grows, so does your toolkit for solutions and ideas. You gain a better sense of what to do at different levels of problems. This keeps you calmly solving issues until a problem arrives that exceeds your level of experience and knowledge.

I have found that the best strategy is to approach new challenges as progressive learning opportunities. In time I began to gain an underlying belief that I could find a solution to the problems that came my way. This way of thinking changed my mindset and perspective, and lowered my stress. Instead of feeling helpless about issues, I began to approach them with fresh energy and excitement to meet the next challenge.

The growth of a company brings issues and situations

of challenge that grow over time. It starts with smaller issues that grow as the company grows. If, however, you learn to progressively deal with problems, the problems that come your way will continue to match your skills and abilities. Bigger issues appear at the same time you've gained a wider range of skills and experience to solve them. So, know that as your issues get bigger, you will be better equipped to meet them.

As you look to other entrepreneurs and business people that you admire, recognize that they are sweating problems and challenges just like you. Their issues may have more zeros, or involve more people, or may be international, but they are struggling too. Their experience masks it better, but it is there. Business ownership is a struggle and challenge all the time. It is not just you.

SECRET 4

CHOICE

———

The beautiful part of being an entrepreneur is that it is all about choice. The beautiful part of owning your own company is that it's your choice. Unlike having a job or employment where many of the parameters of your day and life are dictated to you, owning a company is nothing but choice. You don't believe me, do you? I know it doesn't feel that way.

Think of a chessboard. Business is like a chessboard with all sorts of moving parts. However, in business, every piece on the board can move in any direction to any square. At any time, you can change any of the variables in your company to better suit your market, your desires, and your pocketbook.

I typically get significant pushback here. Owners I have worked with quickly argue that they can't just change the business or change their products, or their pricing or customers. I'm here to tell you they are wrong; and if you're thinking like they do, you're also wrong. The world of business is constantly changing, and that is often ignored. Every day brings new systems, pricing, suppliers, digital platforms, and customers online and offline. The same way that incremental changes can alter an existing operation, incremental change can be used to overhaul a company in any direction you want.

I know a locksmith with the company name Purrr-fect Lock, with an adorable cat in their logo. I asked the owner how he came up with his company name. He said he initially opened a cat daycare business with his wife, but he didn't really like that business so he set up his own locksmith company. Since they'd already incorporated and had the infrastructure, he just transitioned the name. He was also setting up Purrr-fect Photography. Now, maybe that's poor branding, but it does make a point. Businesses can evolve and move in unforeseen directions like chess pieces on a board with no rules about how to move. You can form new brands with new products, suppliers, and customers. All of those choices can create a new future for the business you're starting right now.

Don't wait until you're fed up and hating your own business. Keep your attention on consciously directing it through your decisions to become something you enjoy and profit from each day.

Although the common thinking is that the customer is king, I believe that you as the owner are king. You are the most important person for the business to serve, because without you there wouldn't be a business—not today and not tomorrow. Once you are clear that your business is serving you with enjoyment and cash, then ensure that it's also serving your team. Next to you, your employees are the most important people who benefit from your business. Finally, ensure that your business is serving the customer.

Of course, it is fundamental that serving the customer and the customer experience is key, but in most companies it soon overshadows the business of serving everyone else. So start at the top. When a business serves the owner and the team, the customer automatically reaps the rewards of a good product or service, and feels cared about.

The Hewlett Packard Company originally tried selling bowling foul-line indicators, automatic urinal flushers, and fat-reduction shock machines, before finally becoming a global electronics company (see the book *Built to Last* by Jim Collins and Jerry Porras). If you want to change your company to a donut shop, you can. If you want to move from home entertainment to clothing, you can.

Stay willing to change anything about your business. Success doesn't come from being tied or committed to just one way of doing things. Every aspect of your business can change. You can replace every bad customer, every supplier, change geography, replace your existing staff, close this, open that. It is nothing but choice every day.

At the same time I want to warn you that changing your whole business model doesn't happen in a day. It can take weeks, months, or years. It has to be done with conscious effort over a reasonable period of time to manage the effect on your existing operation.

For example, in my business, we are committed to firing bad clients, but we can't simply fire them at will. We need to identify them and commit to finding a new client to replace the one we let go. Once we have a new client, we politely invite the old client to find another supplier. It is a process that supports our strategy and conviction that we can choose our direction and outcomes if we do so responsibly.

Your business needs to serve your clients to generate cash flow and profit. Your business also needs to serve you. It is something that needs to be reviewed annually at a minimum. Ask yourself: Is the business still something I am passionate about? Is the business still moving in a direction that serves me? If I were to open the shop today, how would I do it differently? Your answers will inform you about whether you are on track or if you need to change. If you do need to make a change, it's best to start today.

SECRET 5

YES, YOU CAN!

———

"Yes, you can!" is a phrase that every single business owner and entrepreneur needs to hear regularly. If you can't find someone willing to tell you this, then call me and add me to your network. I'll tell you what you need to hear.

Managing a business seems daunting, managing staff is overwhelming, finding time for strategy is next to impossible. So, yes, all of the frustrating feelings and struggles you're having are completely in line with business ownership. Many days you probably feel that there must have been a course you missed on good ownership and management. But don't worry, you are on track and you CAN do it.

You may be looking around at other businesses in your area, your city, your circle of friends and thinking, "Everyone else is running such a great company, but I'm struggling every day." Want to know the truth? Every one of them is thinking the same thing about you.

This presumption typically applies to larger companies. A person might think, "Well, her company is so large, she must have it all under control." Nope! The size of a company is absolutely no indication of smooth operation. Often, the larger the business the more chaos that comes with it. Sometimes that size can just mask inefficiency and disorganization better. It is like a duck swimming along—everything looks smooth above the water, but under the surface there's a whole lot of strenuous paddling going on. A larger duck has to move more weight.

Every business needs to be striving all the time to improve. In order to ensure success, you also need to grow as a person. You need to be learning all the time: reading books, subscribing to industry magazines, listening to podcasts, interviewing suppliers and customers, getting a mentor, following online resources. It all makes you better. Your business only improves at the level you do. If you strive to be your best self and you are open to allowing the company to develop, you can do it! Successful business people are all sorts of people from all walks of life. Some are brilliant, some aren't. Some are tall, some are short. Some are more left brain oriented and some more right brain. Don't worry about what a "successful owner" looks like, just strive to be your best self.

"Yes, you can!"

You need to hear these words from your spouse and from your business friends regularly. Every entrepreneur needs voices of encouragement. It's so important because you probably don't believe it yourself. A little voice inside your head is constantly battling this message with phrases and ideas to undermine you. That's why external voices of support are so critical. My good friend Dominic, a great entrepreneur himself, is always there to reassure me and encourage me with these three words, no matter what day or time I call. Find people who will support you in your goals. If need be, hire someone to tell you, "Yes, you can!"

Over time I found that this message started to come from inside. That negative voice inside my head gradually became more positive and supportive. I began to carry it with more certainty, belief, and commitment. Once this gets into your subconscious, it helps direct your success, and brings you the results you desire. You become unstoppable.

"Yes, you can!"

BUSINESS IS FUN

Life is short. So if you are running a company that you don't find fun, it's time to make a change. You have three choices: shut down, sell the business, or find fun in it again.

At my company when things start to bog down in too much seriousness, I tell my staff, "Look, no one is bleeding to death here, let's all find a smile or a laugh, and enjoy this process."

You too can decide to enjoy the process. Take the example of Paddi Lund.

Paddi is a dentist in Australia who got to the point where he hated his business (as many dentists do, with huge depression and suicide rates internationally). He knew that he had to change things or sell his practice and make for the exit. Paddi took a leap, changed his practice name to Happiness Dentistry, and set out to make it just that. He believed that even if his changes failed, at least he was trying to do business the way he wanted.

He centered his practice in hospitality and got to know his patients better. His office now serves great espresso, more than eighty types of tea, and little pastries called Dental Buns. They provide service with a smile and the smiles go all around. His staff love working there and his patients love it. Paddi's practice soon became so busy that he has a long waiting list of referrals. He made his business fun and success chased after him. Oh, and did I mention that he's making five times more money than he used to? Yes, happiness in business breeds success. (You can find out more about Paddi at www.paddilund.com.)

Make the decision today to put fun back into your company. Beer on Friday, ice cream for customers on Wednesday, colored markers for all notes, team meetings with funny hats or outside in a park. There are many ways to inject fun into the daily routine and transform the experience of your business into Happiness Inc. Be bold and outrageous! You will laugh and smile more, and so will your team. Your customers will come back for more and refer others who like your way of doing business with a smile.

SECRET 7

YOU DEFINE OPPORTUNITY

Derek is a business coach in rural Ireland who bought a coaching franchise and was determined to make it work. The franchise hired me to come all the way from Canada to help him get started. Other business coaches I know are based in cities of millions of people with thousands of potential clients. Derek set up shop in the small town of Ennis, the kind of town you can miss if you blink on the way through. It's a small market, to say the least.

On my first day in Ireland, Derek picked me up at the airport and took me on a drive along winding country roads to the little inn he booked for me. "This is the town I am going to focus my business on!" he told me with great excitement. It was all of two city blocks long, and I was immediately worried for Derek and his ambitions.

I knew that business coaches all over the world were challenged to find enough clients in cities a hundred times the size of Ennis. "How many businesses are in this town?" I asked Derek.

He told me that the local chamber of commerce listed 160 businesses in the area, but with a wink, he said he happened to know that there were actually 186. He was confident that capturing ten to fifteen ongoing clients in that group would be easy.

As things turned out, Derek was right. He went on to have a steady list of clients for years and built a very successful business.

This incredible experience showed me that opportunity is really all about mindset. I have seen people fail over and over in market conditions that screamed success. They failed because they didn't truly believe in themselves or their mindset of opportunity. Any number of other coaches who weren't Derek would have failed. They would have only seen the challenge, not the opportunity in that small town. Derek saw nothing but opportunity and made it a reality.

As you identify your opportunities, think about the people you know or others you can connect with who will support your striving. You aren't looking for "yes men," but people who can help you refine your strategy, challenge your thinking, and support you unequivocally.

People too often listen to "experts" with limited scope for what is or isn't an opportunity. But the fact is that experts don't know any more than you about where to find opportunity. They can only make guesses based on their own beliefs and prejudices.

Most people are afraid of opportunity. They only see the risks and challenges. That's why it's important to follow your own instincts and mindset. If you believe you can make something work, you likely can. If you see an opportunity that others don't, then you're probably right. Be courageous and trust yourself, and pursue the opportunities you believe in.

STOP PLAYING TO YOUR STRENGTHS

All too many people in business are busy playing to their strengths. The accountant buries herself in the office to check bookkeeping entries. The outgoing, gregarious owner is busy selling and meeting clients when he has serious inventory and production problems back at the shop.

A mechanic I know couldn't grow his business because every time an issue presented itself, he retreated to the garage and got underneath a car. He was an incredible mechanic and his work was great for his customers, but awful for his staff and company. He either needed to face his role as owner, or hire someone who could.

Highly effective entrepreneurs don't make those mistakes. They play to the needs of their business, not to the skills and strengths they love or are good at. Great entrepreneurs tackle the biggest issues in their business. They make to-do lists that are dead honest about their biggest challenges, and then set to work solving them. They focus on what their business needs, even if it requires the greatest stretch of their skills. They know that if they can solve the biggest issues and toughest challenges in their operations first, then everything else will take care of itself and become manageable. When a challenge is beyond their skills, they don't hesitate to bring in resources to help.

I'm not saying that if you love sales you should stop selling, or if you love production work you should exit production altogether. Spend some time every week doing what you love in your business, but first be sure to prioritize the most important needs of your business.

Take an honest look at the issues in your company. What are your biggest issues right now? If you aren't sure what they are, ask your team or your customers, and be prepared to hear the honest truth. Honest feedback may be tough to hear at first, but it will give you the insight you need to apply your focus. Knowing what needs work, and seeing that it gets done, are the signs of a true entrepreneur.

CREATIVE PROBLEM-SOLVING

———

I used to believe that I wasn't creative. I said to people, "I can't draw a circle, let alone a picture." I avoided Pictionary like the plague. I thought that creativity was the exclusive domain of people talented in the arts. I was missing something.

I became an entrepreneur, and out of necessity I began solving the everyday problems of business. I saw that every issue or challenge had many possible solutions. Each piece of business could move in multiple directions. When people said, "There is no way to fix that," I asked, "Why not? If there is a solution, what would it be?" I discovered that open-minded thinking led to inventive solutions.

One day seemingly out of nowhere, my good friend

Monica told me that I was creative. I had no idea what she meant. "I'm not an artist," I told her. She couldn't understand how I couldn't see it. She explained, "Look, you're able to find solutions to all sorts of situations where other people just throw their hands in the air. You see opportunity and ways to improve things that other people don't even notice. Of all the people I know, if I have a problem that needs to be solved, I know I can come to you and you'll find a way. You are incredibly creative."

It was a powerful realization for me, and it changed my way of thinking about what creativity is and how we can use it. I came to see how I was actually using creativity to solve problems in my companies over and over again.

As it turns out, creativity in problem-solving is a key entrepreneurial trait. In business, creativity applies to innovation in selling, production, marketing, and every other aspect of running a company. Business people regularly embrace creative innovation to develop new tools and better methods to get the job done. Creativity is natural in business and natural to people who are successful in business. Apply your own creativity to problem-solving in your business and you'll find options and solutions you didn't know existed.

SECRET 10

NO EGO

—

Have you ever watched great athletes in interviews? I mean the really great ones like Wayne Gretzky, Jerry Rice, Serena Williams, LeBron James, and many others. These are people who have every right to be cocky, egotistical, and high on themselves about their achievements. But they aren't. They recognize that their success comes from their own hard work, as well as the hard work of their teammates, coaches, support networks, and families. It comes from opportunities they were given, along with some lucky breaks. It's always a pleasure to hear their honest humility, gratitude, and praise of others.

This is exactly how a great business owner, leader, and entrepreneur thinks and operates. You may be the one who owns the company, but success depends on your staff, customers, suppliers, professionals, and the wider community. It's a collective success. Taking time to reflect on who is helping you now, and who helped you to get there, is crucial. It is also important to take steps to acknowledge this help and pay gratitude to it.

Dean, a CEO and my longest-standing friend, began writing personal letters to his team and stakeholders one Christmas. It came out of necessity. Dean's company was a tech start-up with no money for Christmas bonuses, gifts, or even a staff party. So he decided to give each person a handwritten letter about how much he appreciated their personal ideas, efforts, and contribution to the company. The positive feedback was so overwhelming that Dean has continued this tradition for years, even after the business started making money. His staff has grown substantially, and now it takes him weeks of writing, but he still makes it his business to complete each personal, handwritten letter. He continues this expression of gratitude because it means something not only to his staff and stakeholders, but to himself. He wants each individual to know how grateful he is for their hard work and dedication to the company's success, as well as his own.

To create a successful, supportive team you need to demonstrate your willingness to work alongside them every day. You need to put your ego away, because it quickly turns staff off. It's the same with customers. Brand loyalty is generated by companies that care about their clients and put their customers' needs and satisfaction first. There's no room in business for patting yourself on the back.

It's reasonable to recognize your skills and business talents, but it's no cause for chest-thumping. Before you congratulate yourself, make a list of all the people and organizations that support your vision and have contributed vitally to your success.

Set an example of humility, vulnerability, and communal responsibility at your company. On occasion, don't hesitate to empty a wastebasket or clean the counter in the break room. Your role as owner is to be a strategic and focused leader, but it doesn't hurt to walk in others' shoes once in a while. It's a reminder that everyone at every level of the company drives its success.

PASSION FOR EVERYTHING!

———

If you are not absolutely passionate about every aspect of your product, service, team, and customers, then it's time to get out of business. Sell it off or shut it down. You can't operate a business that takes up the majority of your time and the vast majority of your energy and thoughts if you don't feel a burning passion for it.

Yes, there are days when you'd like to burn the business to the ground and collect the insurance money. Days when you want to fire everyone you see—staff and clients. It's normal to feel that way sometimes, even if you love your business. All entrepreneurs are pushed to their limits. In order to weather those tough days, however, you need a deep-seated desire to make it work and a big passion for what you're doing.

I have operated companies where I was very passionate about what we were offering and the impact we were making. I've also gotten into ventures where I wasn't passionate about what we were doing. For me, it's the difference between being in the business with "heart and head" or just with my head. Every successful venture and outcome I've created and stuck with to fruition has been a heart and head venture. Every time I was in business only with my head, the results were mediocre.

Why is passion such a critical piece? It's because passion comes through in everything you do. People can hear it in your voice. They can see it in your walk, and can feel it in your presence. Clients want to buy that passion. Employees want to work with that passion. People are loyal to passion. Most people lack passion in their work lives, so when you have passion you are both a magnet and a generator of passion in others.

Passion is vital to your long-term business success. If you don't have passion, it means you need to make changes in your business, or start a different company entirely. During the life cycle of a business, passion can ebb and flow, or simply die out. You may reach a certain milestone and feel that you've accomplished what you needed to. It is all part of your journey as an entrepreneur. In my experience, however, when I've realized that my passion was depleted, and that my heart had gone out of the business,

I've immediately moved to find a way out. My last decision to exit a company was prompted by my wife, who could see my passion had left me. She pointed out that I was extremely busy, but I didn't seem to be having fun anymore.

How do you know if you have the necessary passion to make your business a success? The simple answer is, if you have to ask, you probably don't. Passion is a feeling of excitement that makes you want to rise to challenges and meet them head-on. You wake at 6 a.m. thinking about work and excited to get up, go out, and do it. It's not an obligation, but an inspiration. Gut-check your passion level every month, and when you confirm it's still there, harness it every day to inspire and create the business you really want.

SECRET 12

ABUNDANCE IS EVERYWHERE

———

Fundamental to the growth of your company is holding fast to the belief of abundance. You need to believe with certainty that there is an abundance of clients, money, time, and resources for your business. Do you hold that belief, or are you not so sure? That difference in mindset can determine your success even before you show up to work.

Ask yourself: do I operate from a position of scarcity or abundance?

At no other time in history has business had such easy access to global markets. Customers and their pocketbooks can be reached online, and goods shipped to even remote locations worldwide. The size of the global middle class is estimated at 3.2 billion people. Finding an abundance of clients is easy and viable. The GDP of countries today is measured in the billions and trillions. That's plenty of cash for businesses to tap into. This is the business environment of abundance we are operating in today.

When you lose a customer, there's a treasure trove of others to reach out to. When cash is tight, you can be sure there's still plenty out there. When you're hiring, you need to know that there's a wealth of talent your company can bring on board. You may not know the details yet of where to access your next client, more cash, or your next great hire, but to do so you must believe in the abundance of resources available to support your success.

Learning to focus on an abundance mindset is a practice and habit you can strengthen. It's like building muscle, but with statistics, facts, and information about your market, your industry, and the wider economy.

Even during the Great Recession of 2008–2009, when sales at my restaurants were off by 43 percent, I still knew that 57 percent of our customers were coming in. I made a conscious decision to focus on the customers we had, instead of the ones who were missing. I knew that if we remained positive and continued to welcome our customers with open arms, the others would return in time.

Instead of breeding an atmosphere of scarcity at our restaurants, I led by modeling an attitude of abundance.

Business is a long game, but it should be played with attention to the short wins and gains. It's like a sports game with each hit, goal, or basket gradually raising the score. Each sale, each new hire, each new order leads to abundance. Get in the habit of seeing the abundance in your world and watch your company grow.

PART TWO

—

VISION BIG

The most profound vision story I can share with you concerns a meeting I had with the owner of a manufacturing company. Steve had been in business for thirteen years. When I asked him what his personal vision had been when starting his company, he caught me by surprise. "I wanted to run my former boss out of business."

"Well, how is that going?" I asked him.

"I did it in eighteen months!"

It was one of the strangest visions for a business I'd ever heard. I offered my awkward congratulations, then asked him, "After meeting that initial goal, what has your vision been since then? What's been driving you for the past eleven and a half years?"

Steve got fidgety, he looked at me then looked away. He stroked his beard. He pushed his chair back. Finally, he said, "Well, I guess what drives me is needing to pay my mortgage."

I was dumbfounded. "That's it? That's your driving motivator and vision for your company?"

"I guess so, I haven't really thought about it," he said. "You're the first person to ask me that question in the last eleven years."

No wonder his business was in trouble. His company had staff retention issues, sales challenges, lack of energy, and a general navigational void in his offices and warehouse. There was no urgency, no striving at this company. It was like a ship afloat without a rudder and no port in sight.

Steve's limited vision of merely paying his home mortgage could hardly inspire his organization and his customers. It didn't motivate his staff to be their best.

Over the months following our initial meeting, I worked with Steve to craft a new vision for where he wanted his business to go. He established that he wanted to be an industry leader with high-quality product at the best prices sourced from China and around the world. He set new goals for sales and quality levels. He engaged his team for input and ideas. Long-standing issues found correction with new tactics and emotional drivers.

Steve's new vision began to give purpose to his people. It brought focus to their work, their departments, and their measure of team performance. It became a strategic beacon to everyone at the company. Even customers began commenting on their recent interactions with staff, saying that order speed and product quality had improved remarkably.

Just as Steve's new vision became the roadmap of his

success, so too can your vision be the inspiration for your company. Vision is an all-encompassing emotional picture of your company's future. That's why it's so important to spend the time to develop your vision in spectacular detail.

For example, how will you design and furnish your office space? What will your product packaging look like? No detail is too small or insignificant for your vision. You may not know the answers immediately, but you can imagine and plan as your vision unfolds. Take time to develop your vision down to the smallest details. Get input from your people, shape your vision carefully, and share it openly. Your vision will inspire your company and drive your success.

VISION, GOALS, MISSION, CULTURE... I'M CONFUSED

———

There seems to be a lot of confusion around the terms vision, goals, mission, and culture. Are all of these guideposts really necessary for success in business?

In my work advising entrepreneurs, I have found that what's most important is (1) a crystal clear, detailed vision for what you're creating, (2) a defined culture for your organization, and (3) a "Big Hairy Audacious Goal" or BHAG.

I don't include mission statements in the mix because they are generally too static, too formal, and have little passion. A mission statement seems to be something created in a strategic afternoon workshop by the company executive. It gets printed and placed in the reception area, and no one ever looks at it again. Of course, some organizations have fine mission statements that serve as guides for the entire company, but the average staffer, when asked, can't remember it. So don't waste your time crafting a mission statement unless it is profound, bold, and memorable.

On the other hand, vision is an entrepreneur's essential piece of guidance and inspiration. Vision is a personal picture with depth, color, texture, energy, and real feeling. It's something that can live in your mind and you can bring to fruition with significant power to motivate others.

For example, if you were going to open a bakery, your vision would include the aroma of fresh bread baking. Imagine the heady scent of baked goods greeting your customers as they enter the front door. Your vision includes people standing three deep at the counter at 8 a.m. as staff hands out samples of fresh raisin bread. How does it taste? Warm, sweet, and delicious. The vision you imagine in your mental picture becomes your internal guide to the business you bring to reality.

The second key piece to your company's strategic success is creating a rock-solid, intensely defined culture. We'll take a deep dive into culture later in the "People" section of this book, but what's important to remember is that a company's culture defines how everyone at every level of an organization acts, operates, and excels. Culture determines how staff interact on the job with each other and with customers. Company culture brings people to a healthy, ethical place as a group with common goals.

The "Big Hairy Audacious Goal" or BHAG is a phrase coined by authors Jim Collins and Jerry Porras in the classic business book, *Built to Last*. BHAG is the third essential piece of the high-level puzzle. In almost all organizations, the staff don't have their own goals for the company. They need leadership to define a goal that they can rally around and buy into. Unlike vision, which looks long into the future, goals are generally short term and can change. An achievable BHAG might be that a company hits a specific sales target. That Big Hairy Audacious Goal can be made more exciting with a reward in the end, such as everyone going to NASCAR in celebration. That's a concrete goal to work toward!

A furniture store owner I advised had a long-term vision of a chain of stores, and a clear picture of how she would run them. As part of her vision, she saw herself living her winters in a warm climate. Her vision was too personal to engage and inspire her staff, so she focused them on achievable short-term BHAGs, goals with clear direction. One year it was a sales figure that was dramatically higher than anything they had achieved before. The goal was tied to a reward: the store would be closed for five days and the entire staff would vacation in Las Vegas, all expenses paid. They constantly tracked their sales, talked about and shared their plans for what the Vegas trip would include. The BHAG really got the team fired up, the same way the owner's personal vision worked for her. The team shattered previous sales levels and they all went to Las Vegas!

Another retailer I worked with had a very clear vision of customer experience. Much like the bakery vision described earlier, this owner imagined every detail of a customer's interaction with his company. He shared his vision with each staff member on the day they joined his company, and spoke of his vision almost daily. His vision was the driving force for team training, all decisions, and customer interactions. Yet he found that it wasn't quite enough to continually motivate his staff.

So, with a little guidance, the retailer set out to define a specific short-term BHAG for his team. He decided on a lofty goal, which was to be the number one company in their market based on sales, number of stores, and customer satisfaction ratings. He was so passionate about this goal that it "infected" and inspired the staff. People monitored their progress on the BHAG each quarter, and celebrated their gains every time they moved closer to their ultimate goal. They coupled their short-term goal to the owner's long-term vision and together they brought their goal across the finish line.

You and your team should be guided by your company's vision, culture, and goals. As a team, people need to know what they are creating and why. It can be intensely personal. It can be about community. It can be about some greater good or deep pride in shared work. It can be about higher sales, customer outreach, common values, and mutual objectives. What's important is that the entire team be motivated and committed to the kind of organization you want to create. Make it personal for them too, and you'll be absolutely amazed at how much effort and commitment people will bring to your company.

WEEKLY RENEWAL

The most common issue with a company's vision is that it doesn't stay active on a daily basis. It's like a misplaced business plan that ends up on a shelf, never to be looked at again.

When I ask business owners about their vision, I often hear, "Oh, I have it on my computer somewhere, can I email it to you?"

Days later I receive it and have a look. I tell them, "This is excellent. It's inspiring!" Then I ask them how often they review the vision, and they say, "Well, never really."

That's the problem. A company's vision needs constant renewal. It's the guiding picture of what you're building. Your vision is your muse, your inspiration, and your roadmap. You need to be considering it daily, or if not daily, then weekly. Your vision should lift your spirits and provide guidance, direction, and motivation to your entrepreneurial dreams. It is an internal and external tool.

A visionary entrepreneur doesn't start off his or her week like most other people, arriving at the office, getting some coffee, and going right to their email. Instead, you start your week by reviewing and imagining your business. You find a neutral third place between your home and workplace, perhaps a favorite coffee shop or diner, where you can sit and quietly review your vision. I go to a terrific coffee shop called the Purple Perk, where they bake incredible Morning Glory muffins. I launch my week with terrific coffee, a warm muffin, and no distractions from my vision and goals for my own little "empire."

After you've fired up your week by taking stock of your vision, you can show up at your workplace with your vision renewed. In this way, you'll know how to direct your people. You'll know what you need them to accomplish both short and long term. You'll be able to see to the far horizon, way past the distraction of emails. By planning your steps and actions for the week you'll bring your vision that much closer to fruition. This is how you transform your vision into daily action.

FROM 40,000 FEET TO GROUND LEVEL

———

If I had one business superpower, it would be the ability to think about a business at a 40,000-foot strategic level, then bring it down to the tactical ground level of what to do today. I call it a superpower, because that's how difficult it seems to plan at the highest level of strategy and then return effectively to the ground level of tactics. Yet that's exactly what entrepreneurs must do.

At 40,000 feet, an entrepreneur is thinking five to ten years out, looking to see where the industry and the world is going. What trends will have influence? How will AI change the industry? What innovations in production are coming down the pike? What emerging markets might fit the business? How will the business adapt to meet next-generation client expectations?

Coming down to 30,000 feet, the entrepreneur is using those future insights to create a guiding strategy that can tangibly steer the company forward. They are defining goals and objectives that are going to be the foundational directions and beacons for the business. They are starting to move those goals to broad strategic steps that will need to be planned in advance. These could involve committing to new geographies, a new product line, more automation for manufacturing, online customer service, and other broad directional strategies for the business.

At 20,000 feet, the entrepreneur is setting priorities to narrow down all possible strategies to zero in on what is essential. Is rebranding critical for the overall marketing strategy? What pieces of the company's technology need to change in the next twelve months to sell in the global marketplace? At what speed and priority will new hires be made?

At 10,000 feet, the entrepreneur is compartmentalizing and considering immediate adjustments to each area of the business. How to best unify the team? How does manufacturing meet new cost challenges? How does the company expand its customer base and maximize the customer experience? How does the company become a stronger digital marketer?

At 5,000 feet, the entrepreneur starts to rough out

monthly, weekly, and daily tactics to address each area of the company for delivery or innovation. This involves drilling down to all the major areas of the business, from finance and marketing, to service, delivery, sales, and people, then looking at specific actions and tactical improvements to take now.

At 1,000 feet, the entrepreneur is fine-tuning and scheduling items for implementation and adjustment. Those of the highest priority are budgeted and moved to an execution calendar (timeline) with detailed steps and assignments to complete. Other ideas are kept on a back burner for now. As items are completed, others may be reprioritized, and the next highest priorities are scheduled for execution.

At ground level, the rubber hits the road: it's time to execute with focus!

SECRET 16

QUAKING ASPEN TREES

———

Researchers who study trees have recently found that aspen trees, those "trembling giants" with the highest peaks, actually behave as a single living organism with one massive underground root system. It's a striking discovery, and interestingly, one that relates directly to the structure of a business.

A business operates and grows in ways very similar to the aspen tree root system. The many aspects of business—sales, marketing, finance, administration, service, delivery—are all interconnected and operate in concert with one another. Each affects the other, so that a change made in one area will influence the entire system.

An increase in sales will affect business finances, cost of goods, and changes in inventory. Increase in demand is reflected in increases in production, which in turn may increase your labor requirement, administration, and paperwork. A sale is not simply about sales, it reverberates throughout every area of the business.

Business experts and educators talk about business as though it is a series of silos. Sales is thought to exist unto itself in its own separate silo, as does administration and finance. HR is the company's people resource and your organization's lifeblood, yet it is also thought to reside in its own silo. Process and manufacturing, technology systems and marketing (wait, is marketing different from sales?) all seem to exist apart from each other.

This breakdown of business structure into functional areas of specialty and focus can make sense for understanding the components of a business. However, it doesn't make sense on the level of business dynamics, because all the pieces are actually moving parts that interact in relationship together. All of these areas are linked as one giant organism and need to communicate with each other. As you move, adjust, or change any area of the business, there is a ripple effect in every other aspect of the business too.

A great exercise for understanding this basic business reality is to make a change to a single point or variable in your business, and then track the effects and subsequent reverberations in other areas. You can do this alone or with your team, as a real-life change or simply a discussion exercise. Doing this regularly can give everyone at your company a deeper understanding of true business dynamics. At first you might find five ways in which a single change impacts other areas. Months later you may see a more far-reaching impact across the business from a single change. Moving one piece can spread through your company's root system to the entire living, breathing organism that is your company.

To successfully operate, manage, and grow a company, it's important to understand and respect this interconnectedness. The more deeply you understand your business in this way, the better you can move between thinking about a specific area of the business and its connection across the company. You'll be able to simultaneously focus attention on details while seeing the larger implications companywide. This will help you develop more dynamic control over your company's potential and success.

A LIVING PLAN

"Woah! Look at the dust on this thing!"

That's what I heard one day from a business owner taking a professionally written, $35,000 business plan off his office shelf. He hadn't looked at it in years. I read it from front to back and told him that it contained some very solid, effective ideas.

"Yeah it might, I don't remember," he said.

If that was his attitude, why had he spent so much money for a business plan he wasn't using? The answer is that he thought it was a static document to be read once, presented to his investors, and then put away for eternity.

He had it all wrong. A business plan is more than financial projections that remain stagnant. Just like your company vision, a business plan is a guide that needs constant monitoring, updating, and revising. Your business is an ever-changing organic being, and so is your business plan. As one of your primary tools, your plan needs to change and adapt over time to conditions on the ground.

How many entrepreneurs actually carve out consistent time weekly and monthly to strategically review, measure, and plan the future of their business? In my experience, it's no more than 5 percent, but they are the business owners that are killing it in their industries and far exceeding most other companies' performance.

Updating your business plan requires a certain degree of balance. You update the plan as a response to results you're getting in the market and what you project for the future. You don't update the plan every time things get hard. You don't reduce your expectations or soften your goals. It's not a daily update. You are careful not to react to trends or to your emotional bumps and stresses. That's where balance comes in.

Review your plan weekly and monthly, focusing beyond just today. Revise the plan each quarter, updating details as part of your active strategic management. This ensures that your plan is balanced, so that it's static enough to use, but dynamic enough to be alive and malleable.

Make your business plan a "living" plan. Schedule quiet

strategy time in your calendar for managing your plan. Block time in your schedule for the highest level of review, insight, and planning. This is critical to your long-term success. Some owners argue that they can't leave their business operations and the issues of today to just go "think" about the business. I've heard all the excuses for not scheduling time to review the direction of their business.

What they don't realize is that they are missing out on the strategic confidence that comes from evaluating and making adjustments to the big picture. A strong, dynamic business plan anchors a business owner to the long view, playing out in day-to-day operations.

The entrepreneurs I work with find that as they get in the habit of managing their living business plan, their enthusiasm grows and they look forward to the time they devote to it. It's like a refueling. This coincides with the practice of reviewing your vision for the business. The revisiting of your vision ensures that inspiration is still your true north. Revisiting your business plans ensures that you're traveling toward it. Your regular connection to these essentials is crucial when day-to-day challenges and problems risk pulling you from your path and your plan. So, update your business plans regularly to create the incredible business you've always pictured, and the life you deserve.

RIGHTSIZE YOUR COMPANY

In North America, businesses are driven by the cycles of publicly traded companies. We measure everything based on performance every ninety days. Continuous nonstop growth is valued at all costs. It's all designed to drive sales, profits, and beat the last result. The market won't accept less in a quarter, it always wants more.

As a business owner and entrepreneur, you aren't responsible to the public markets. You therefore don't need to follow or buy into the prevailing pressures of continuous growth. I often meet with entrepreneurs who are feeling poorly about their business' performance because it's not setting growth records every quarter. They presume that continuous record growth is the defining measure of success. That's not always the case. It all depends on how large or small you envision your business to be.

Bo Burlingham's terrific book *Small Giants* gives some outstanding examples of how entrepreneurs found other metrics and guidelines for establishing how their companies operated. They shook off the presumed expectations and grew beyond just sales and profits. They shed the notion that bigger was always better.

One owner decided to stop hiring and growing his company when he realized that he no longer knew all of his employees' names. He realized that personally knowing his people was critically important to him. Relationships mattered more than sales growth.

The owner of a deli business realized that opening other stores or franchising was going to impact the quality and control of their products (sandwiches). So they decided to maximize the business at a single store. It eliminated travel, reduced administration costs, gave them more control of the business, and reinforced connection with their customers.

What is the right size for your company?

The key word here is "right." Smaller isn't always better, nor is bigger. It's all about personal preference. As a business owner, you need to feel empowered to measure success with metrics that matter to you, not the standard expectations.

If you are restricting the nature of growth in your business, turning down opportunities to grow because you don't feel comfortable with it, then you need to look at the why behind those decisions. Is it really about rightsizing your operation, or are there other factors at play? Some business owners feel intimidated by growth and fear getting in over their heads. Others are sometimes driven toward growth at great personal cost to themselves and their families. People have different personalities and visions for success. What's yours?

It's important to know that you have the ability to define, create, and rightsize your organization at any time. You can decide to define your metrics for performance and success at the start-up stage or later as an established business.

I personally like it when healthy financial metrics (the standard everyone uses to measure business performance) are combined with new metrics that are more personal and experiential. Review your profit margin at the end of every quarter. Then review your team engagement numbers, your customer ratings, and even your Google reviews. It's empowering to know that you're making a profit, impacting people, and can choose how large you grow. Having that control is a significant part of being an entrepreneur.

ALWAYS CHOOSE QUALITY

—

Quality is important to me. A sweater made of quality wool. Food with quality ingredients. A car with quality design and finishing. Quality is inspiring. It lifts my enjoyment of everything. There is an element of luxury and care that comes with quality. There is also an element of self-respect attached to it. I know that the company or person that crafted a quality item really took pride in it.

Quality can be part of your vision. Do you want your company to be known for the highest-quality product or service in your space? Not only do high-quality competitors consistently charge more, but they make more money and have better reputations (think of Mercedes, Rolex, or Ben and Jerry's). They are highly motivated to innovate and create better processes and culture. A quality commitment to what you produce ensures a commitment to building a quality business with a vision to match.

The easiest way to enter a market can be with the cheapest, lowest-quality goods. Think of Hyundai and Kia. They both entered the car market with the cheapest, simplest, poorest-quality products to capture the bottom end of the market and their little piece of market share. Within two years, however, they started to raise the quality and price of their cars to capture a share of the mid-market. Now they are producing high-quality models to compete in the higher luxury end of the market (but still at the lowest price for a luxury vehicle).

What this business model demonstrates is that sometimes, in order to get into a busy marketplace, you need to start at the low end. But don't stay there! Once you have market share, it's a whole lot easier and smarter to penetrate the higher end of the market as well. To do so, however, you must embrace quality.

How well is your company competing when it comes to quality and price? Are you at the lower end of the market and content to stay there? Or are you eager to move your company upmarket? If you provide a service, you can make that move up by adding a gold or platinum service option to your existing customer options. If you provide a product, you can manufacture something at the higher end and charge a higher price for it. Delivering quality to the marketplace will inspire your staff to improve processes, create a higher standard, and ultimately make more money for the company.

Oh, and did I mention that customers will love your products and company more? People brag about their favorite things and places because of the positive emotional impact they have in their lives. Sure, people also brag about great deals, but it's usually when they bought a quality product from a reputable company for a reasonable price. No one goes to a dollar store, buys some piece of junk for seventy-five cents, and then raves about it to their friends. Doesn't happen. You don't want to be the one trying to make that happen in your business.

When you consider the products and experiences *you* love, what characteristics make an impact on you? Write these down and then challenge yourself to bring those characteristics to your product or service. Build quality into your vision.

I love it when a business treats me well, like a hotel chain that rewards frequent guests with VIP rates, exclusive services, or a personalized surprise. As a business owner, it makes me think about how my company can reach out to clients regularly to thank them and let them know what they mean to us. Build quality into your operation, implement it, and systemize it. It's the surest way to grow your business. Start your move toward high quality. Your pride and your wallet will thank you!

CHOOSING AN INDUSTRY

How do you decide which industry to be in? How do you decide what product you want to represent or create? Success in business usually goes hand in hand with your values and interests. A product or service that captures your imagination and moves you emotionally is the surest way to go.

You've heard it before: Don't just go after something you think will make a lot of money. A business choice made just on financial considerations isn't enough to sustain an entrepreneur through all the ups and downs of daily operations and the long-term struggles of a business. While following the money might work short term, passion provides the resilience an entrepreneur needs to stay the course.

My longtime friend Dom and I spoke recently about choosing our next business to pursue. Dom had sold his share of an online retailer for a tidy sum. When I asked him what interested him now, he said without hesitation, "A coin-operated car wash."

His reply took me completely off guard. "Why?" I asked him.

"It's cash-based, it's simple, and it has low people requirements. It can run long hours, and since I live in a moderate climate, it can stay open year-round."

"Is that how you choose a business?" I asked.

"Yes," he said, and then he asked me, "What business do you want to get into next?"

"I'd like to own a vineyard, a chain of flower shops, and a boutique hotel."

Dom was dumbfounded. "Why choose those?"

I said, "I love wine and I'd be able to get all of my vintages for free. I love fresh flowers in the house every day. I also love a good hotel experience, and I think it would be cool to try my hand at it."

"So that's how you pick a business to pursue?!" Dom gasped.

It's clear that we were pursuing different approaches to selecting a business. However, we were also using the same model: choosing what would satisfy our highest values. For Dom it was simplicity, consistency, and low headache. For me it was experience, love of product, and quality. Both are right.

You need to know that the business you choose meets your highest values. You also want to be sure that your interest in it can sustain you long term. You can be successful in almost anything if it matches your values and level of interest.

You'll need to break into your industry's market, so you'll need to meet all the functional requirements of your product or service. You'll need financial management, strong delivery, good sales, and marketing. Starting out with a business that aligns with your values and interests is key, as is mastering the functional skills necessary for running the business.

What if you've already committed to a business that you don't love, don't value, and feel stuck in?

I see two options for you: (1) apply your values and passions to that business, or (2) get out of the business (even at a loss, because you can always make more money, but you can't recover time spent in a business you dislike).

For example, consider the insurance industry. Most people I know in insurance simply fell into it. Few, if any, had a passion for insurance when they were growing up. Now they sell and deliver insurance coverage, but let's say their real passions tend more toward personal relationships and technological innovations. Their values don't necessarily connect directly to the products they sell, so if they choose to remain in the insurance industry, they'll need to tie their interests and passions to the business.

An insurance company executive who values personal relationships can focus on the needs of customers and seeing that those needs are met by quality insurance coverage as their base level of service. They can add gold-standard service programs, promote health screenings, social events with clients, and other customer service initiatives. An executive who is technologically savvy can bring leading-edge software, mobile apps, cloud computing, and AI to benefit the customer experience and level of coverage.

On the other hand, an insurance company owner who simply can't find value or interest in their industry needs to sell and get out. You can't succeed long term in a business where you have no interest and no enjoyment.

In my experience, many entrepreneurs have simply lost focus on what they value, and are not conscious of bringing their highest interests to their existing operation. If they can start to identify and reflect more on their values, they can get their passion back with positive results. If they do, here are some of the results they'll see:

- Interest in their business goes up
- Delivery and quality improve
- Staff becomes more engaged
- The business attracts more customers who appreciate new services
- Staff and customer retention improves

Remember to choose your next venture wisely. Never compromise on what you value and what interests you. Bring your passions to your experience of being an entrepreneur.

SECRET 21

STAY THE COURSE, PIVOT LESS

My first business was in interactive voice response (IVR) software, and later audio production. Like many start-up companies with no reputation, we had trouble getting traction. Sales were a struggle and creating momentum seemed impossible.

As the pressure and frustration of slow sales took hold, my business partner Greg began looking for new applications of our technology and new products we could sell. I would come in on Monday morning and there would be pieces of equipment all over the boardroom table—wires, wood, hammers—it looked like a science fair project. I'd ask, "What's all this?"

He'd say, "I was thinking that if we started to build these

in large quantities, we could move into this new market where there's lots of opportunity."

Over several years, we explored dozens of "new markets" and enough prototypes to fill a *Storage Wars* locker.

The problem wasn't our lack of clever ideas. We, particularly Greg, had lots of those. Our problem was avoidance. It's the reason so many start-ups and struggling companies are constantly pivoting. They aren't getting traction, so they decide it must be easier in a different market, or with a different product.

This common struggle overlooks one important facet of business, which is that entering any new market is tough, really tough. Making sales takes twice as long as you initially think it will. First-generation products often have feature and function gaps. It's extremely hard to find a client base.

The solution is to buckle down, work harder, and not pivot away from your vision and plan.

Pivoting is a trendy way to say "not succeeding." Tech companies love this description because it masks their struggle and failings. In many cases, the problem isn't in the product or service, but in not recognizing the level of effort required to accelerate and succeed in your market.

Becoming a market player, let alone a market leader, takes substantially more effort than most people want to accept. A competitor who is already in your new market, needs to apply much less effort to simply stay there. Getting a foothold in a new industry space is a monumental undertaking.

In our first business, we didn't need another new prototype or a different market. What we needed to do was put more effort into sales. We needed more commitment to the product we had already built. Instead of deviating from our initial vision and plan, we needed to become a better competitor with the products we had.

Eventually we did. We introduced pricing that was better than the largest market player. We introduced new features to our service and launched a 100 percent money-back guarantee (that we had to act on only once in five years). We utilized new technology from outside our market that was substantially better. We developed our sales skills and hired seasoned salespeople. These changes and efforts won us sales and made us more competitive. Eventually we gained strong market share and became number two in our market.

Your first instinct may be to pivot away from your vision and look beyond your product or service. Resist that impulse and respond by asking, "Have I maximized and innovated everything I can? Is there any way I could be more competitive? What skills or product improvements do I need to advance?"

Exhaust the innovation in your current product. Outwork the competition. Only then can you effectively know if your company needs to pivot. It's more likely that by then you'll have found success.

PART THREE

—

SELL, SELL, SELL

The most important thing you can do every day in your business is sell something. I have to say that again: THE most important thing you can do every day in your business is sell something.

Everything starts with a sale, and I mean *everything*. If you can keep sales going, all the rest of your business will work itself out. Of course, it's not quite so simple. If you sell 1,000 widgets, you need to have a system in place to get them delivered. Everything in your organization must be positioned to deliver customer satisfaction on sales.

From this moment onward, think of yourself as not only an entrepreneur and business owner, but as the head salesperson. When you embrace sales as the key to success, so will everyone else in your organization. Your identity as the master salesperson of your company has the power to shift sales performance across your entire enterprise.

I met with an entrepreneur who had raised hundreds of thousands of dollars from friends and family. He'd been refining his prototype for more than six years and was on version forty-three of his product. He was busy estimating production capacity, looking at warehouse space, and considering a new loan for more production equipment. His organization chart had changed hundreds of times, and he'd spent the last nine months conducting interviews for staff positions. He was still working on a pay scale that would maximize profits.

I had one question for him: "What have you sold so far?"

His answer was nothing, zero, nada. While he was busy trying to manage all the variables of his business, he hadn't actually sold anything.

As kindly as I could, I told him that he didn't really have a business yet, but he argued adamantly that he did. "Look," I said, "until someone buys something, you have nothing but a volunteer hobby."

So he kicked me out of his garage.

When I saw him a year later, he was working a new job in construction. He had spent all of his start-up money working through the endless variables without ever getting to market and completing a transaction. Unfortunately, he never got to experience the thrill of people buying the product he envisioned.

Sales is the drumbeat of a company. When sales are great, a business has choices and options. It can be opportunistic and future-focused. When sales are poor, every area of a company feels the stress and strain. It's therefore vital that the entire team hears the drumbeat, regardless of their role in the business, and that each team member supports sales in any way they can.

An organization that masters sales is positioned to thrive and enjoy the ride. Remember, you don't truly have a business until you embrace sales as your organization's focus and lifeblood.

EVERYONE SELLS FOR SUCCESS

—

Can your receptionist explain what your business does? Other than your sales team, can any of your staff make an elevator pitch for your company?

The answer to both questions should be yes. Everyone at your company needs to be able to explain what your business does, confidently, concisely, and sincerely. Every person you employ interacts with different people socially, online, and across networks. Each one of them should be able to proudly say, "I work for the greatest company in the world and (what we do, make, or provide) is..." You get the idea?

In our connected world, every team member has ample opportunity to promote and explain the business where they spend their work life. You have a built-in team of promoters. Your employees are a natural resource you need to use. Make it known to the people in your organization that you encourage them to spread the good word about the work you do together. The stronger your culture and the more focused your company message, the more likely it will be that staff will buy in and share messaging with others in their social networks.

It's not just saying where they work or in what industry, but providing testimonials about the company, its products or services, and what makes it special. Each employee has their own way of communicating, and that's good. Their messaging needs to be heartfelt and enthusiastic, expressed in a way that is true to themselves. It's the kind of passionate messaging that creates customers—and sales.

The test of a good elevator pitch is the emotional reaction to it. It should be "WOW!"

It's not about "selling" people, but about telling the story of where they work and why. It's about honestly communicating meaning and purpose in their work. Do your people love working for your organization? Are they proud to be delivering a superior product or service? If they can't muster the excitement, it's important to ask yourself, "Am I creating an environment where people love to work? Am I heading a company that empowers and inspires its staff? Am I building a company culture that supports and motivates its people?" If not, then you have to change the way you do business. If you are creating an inspiring culture, but some staff members aren't responding, then maybe they are at the wrong company.

The way in which staff do their jobs also sells your business. Harry Beckwith, author of *You, Inc.*, tells a fantastic story about interviewing for a job at a marketing agency. He didn't get the job, but sixteen months later he was back at the agency on behalf of one of his own clients. He entered the lobby and the receptionist greeted him, "Hello Harry!"

He was amazed that she remembered his name more than a year after meeting him. He was so impressed by the company culture she represented that he negotiated a $16 million marketing contract with the agency. Now, that's the kind of staff member who makes sales!

OLD-SCHOOL SELLING

—

Are you bombarded with emails every day trying to sell you on some product or service? Is your inbox constantly spammed by the new face of lazy selling? Massive blasts and anonymous emails are based on a misconception that immense volumes of communications get results. The success rate of this kind of selling is more like.oo1 percent and should be avoided at all costs.

Let's talk about how you *should* be selling in your organization.

Your competitors may be looking for the easiest, fastest, and most disconnected way to sell, but I'm here to tell you that they're way off base. Selling platforms may have changed, but people haven't. At the end of the day, customers are still drawn to the same things as always: honest communication; quality products and services that meet their needs; worthwhile connections; and being heard, listened to, and understood.

Here are the proven and profitable sales methods in order of importance:

1. Face-to-face contact
2. Telephone conversation
3. Voicemail
4. Written letters and physical packages
5. Text messages or instant messaging
6. Email

Some people will differ on the most effective order of importance. For example, there's always someone out there claiming to get thousands of responses from emails each week. On the face of it, that sounds too good to be true. Every sales method can generate *some* response, but successful salespeople need the kind of quality connections that lead directly to sales.

Sales pros and business owners who know how to sell are the kind of people who make personal connections, get in front of people every day, have meaningful conversations, and lay the groundwork for sustainable, predictable sales.

Email blasts don't stand up to the kind of human connection that converts to sales. Let's say you send out an email, get a response, then arrange a phone call, invite that prospect to a webinar, set a meeting time, and then try to close the sale. That's a long path to an eventual personal meeting. So why not start with the intention of getting that meeting upfront as your first objective?

When I ask successful entrepreneurs what their sales secret is, they don't tell me, "A website landing page where people fill out order forms any time of day or night." They are all looking for the human touch. No matter their age, they tell me that sales hang on personal connections in person or by phone. They make personal visits, drop in on clients, and book as many one-on-one meetings as they have time for in a week.

They call it "old school."

So stop looking for the easiest way to sell, and focus instead on the most effective. "Press the flesh," as my father and grandfather, both exceptional salesmen, would say. Train yourself and your staff to embrace the old school, get personal, and enjoy the sales success that comes with it.

SHORTEST LINE TO YES

Why do so many companies and people make it hard to buy?

My good friend Dom took me car shopping one day. We test drove an SUV that he and his wife were considering. Dom liked it so much that we detoured to pick her up, and by the end of the test drive they both loved it. We got back to the dealership and Dom said flat out, "I like this car and I'd like to buy it, what's the price?" You can't be more committed to a sale than that.

The salesman said he couldn't just provide the price, but Dom could make an offer. Dom told him that he'd like to make an offer, but he couldn't without having some idea of the asking price. "Just tell me the price and I'll pay it," he said. It went back and forth like that until Dom got angry and offered $1. The salesman said it needed to be a reasonable offer, then he explained that the dealership had a policy to not give out the price, in case the customer went across the street to another dealership to barter. Dom would have been happy to buy at any reasonable price the salesman offered, but the dealership's process got in the way. He wound up not buying the car, but he did stop by the sales manager's office to recommend that they fire the salesman.

Of course the moral of the story is that when someone wants to buy, drop your process, drop your policy, and just say, "Yes!" Get the paperwork going, or walk over to the POS terminal and ring the sale up with a big smile. Your team needs to know that helping people buy when they want to buy is critical to doing business. Sounds easy, but it's rarely taught or discussed in most businesses.

In doing sales coaching and sales shadowing around the world, I've found that most salespeople and business owners get so caught up in the steps of their selling process that they forget to simply listen to the customer and help the buyer buy. The customer says, "This looks like what I need," and the salesperson responds, "Why don't I let you think about it" or "Let's book another meeting" or "Let me show you two more options." Recognize that buyers and customers don't always stand up cheering, "Yes!" when they decide. It's more subtle. They nod their head unconsciously, they say it "looks good," or they ask what the warranty is when they buy.

Learn to read the buying signs and have a process that makes it easy for the buyer. Shorten the sales process where you can by eliminating any steps that serve your staff, the admin, or the finance department and not the customer. When the customer is ready, immediately finish the sale and stop sabotaging your success!

MOST SALESPEOPLE AREN'T

It amazes me that so many people who say they are in sales really aren't. They are in the business of order taking, account management, or professional socializing, but none of these are true sales roles.

There are three lessons that every person in sales needs to know:

1. Don't tell yourself you're selling if all you're doing is talking to the same customers and "following up" on the same six prospects you had a year ago.
2. Don't allow your sales team to tell you they're selling if all they're doing is professional socializing.
3. Most salespeople make their best sales pitch when they interview for their sales job.

Salespeople need to have clear goals and objectives for the first weeks and months of their employment. These include real activity and targets for action. By month three, they should have begun to meet their initial goals for achieved sales and a pipeline of new prospects. Those first three months are a probationary period, and before it runs out, a business should be satisfied that it's made the right hire.

My grandfather was from Kentucky with a big southern drawl and a bold personality. He sold cars for twenty-seven years as a salesman, sales manager, and finally as general manager of a dealership. Here's what he told me about new sales staff: "I'd tell those boys that they needed to sell ten cars in their first month, and if they didn't get them sold, they needed to just come drop off their keys on the corner of my desk. I didn't want to talk to them about it. Just sell the cars or drop off the keys."

Knowing how kind my grandfather was, I asked him, "Didn't you give them a second chance if they sold seven cars? Didn't you see people with potential?"

He shook his head. "I knew that if they didn't sell ten cars out of the gate, they weren't going to suddenly sell ten cars six months from now. I've seen too many people who claimed to be good salesmen, but weren't." Enough said.

Either you're a strong salesperson or you're not. Everyone can improve, but the basics of good sales starts on day one, not a year into the job. Success in sales requires being a pioneer and leader in new markets and networks, new regions and industries. Real salespeople aren't receiving inbound orders every day; they are going out and finding those orders. Real salespeople are generating business from first-time buyers, their existing networks, and more business from existing customers. They are creating and sourcing solutions for their clients. Real salespeople originate, own, and maintain fruitful, ongoing customer relationships.

In order to grow your company, you need to be doing real sales work. You need to be talking to new people, companies, and industries that haven't heard of you and your business. You need to be exploring new buyer territory.

Your salespeople need to be doing the same thing. They should also be compensated according to their ability to generate new sales and open new doors. New clients should be showing up on your weekly sales reports.

New salespeople should be able to make a sale in their first thirty days on the job. If they can't, then terminate them quickly, because you're being bamboozled. Nothing draws on cash like sales salaries and expenses without new sales.

LEADERSHIP SELLING

———

Most people hate salespeople. I secretly love them, but I'm unusual. In our culture, there's a deeply ingrained emotional distaste for the traditional, high-pressure, "sleazy" approach to sales. Customers therefore don't have much trust in salespeople, don't expect to have good interactions with them, and would just rather not.

It's no wonder that many business owners are dreadfully conscious of not wanting to be perceived as slick or pushy when it comes to sales. They also don't want their staff to operate that way.

So, who do people trust?

People trust a leader. Yet the words "leadership" and "sales" are rarely used in the same sentence. This needs to change, because effective selling requires trusted leadership.

Buying decisions are actually solutions to problems: whether the problem is what to wear, what to eat, or what car to drive. People absolutely want someone they trust who can lead them to solutions. They want someone who will give them the facts, lead them through the options, answer their questions, provide clarity, and point a path forward. They want a leader.

With this approach in mind, I created a sales program called Leadership Selling. The basis of the program is that if you operate as a leader by adhering to the principles—Lead. Guide. Help.—people will buy from you all day long. Shoppers who are seeking a product or service want just enough information to make a rational decision. Buyers tend to be nervous and cautious when considering a purchase, especially large ones. They appreciate someone who will lead, guide, and help them process the information they need without pressure.

Imagine the immediate difference in referring to yourself or your sales team as Sales Leaders or Sales Guides, instead of salespeople. It's a conceptual change that can instantly alter your team's approach to sales, the perception of prospective clients, and your business results. It means you are coming from a place of leading people through a proven process of making a successful decision, guiding them to different options, and helping them reach a solution that fits them best.

Try it, and find out more about Leadership Selling at www.evolvebusinessgroup.com/leadershipselling.

SELL THE MERCEDES

———

Ideally, what car does everyone want to own? The best car in the industry, a Mercedes Benz. What wristwatch does everyone want to wear? A Rolex. What ice cream do they prefer? Ben and Jerry's.

Everyone secretly wants the best. So, when it comes to quality, pricing, and sales, the question to ask yourself is: Am I selling the best?

Many new business owners are insecure about competing in the marketplace, and they transfer that insecurity to their pricing. They set their prices too low, hoping to beat the competition. All too often they don't have the confidence to bring a superior product to market at the price it's truly worth. This makes it hard to get good margins and cash flow. New businesses can wind up inadvertently sabotaging themselves by not having enough cash to improve and grow the company.

Once you've entered the market at the bottom end of the price spectrum, it's a long, slow haul to reposition your product or service closer to the top. You've already defined your brand as cheap, economical, and average. Of course, car companies like Kia and Hyundai entered the market with low-end, economical models, then successfully moved into the middle bracket (see Secret 19), but they had to spend millions on advertising and rebranding to reposition themselves. Repositioning can require massive budgets and long timelines that small- and medium-sized businesses just don't have.

If you've already positioned your product near the bottom end of your market, it's time to start raising your prices incrementally. At the same time, you need to build a case for why your product or service deserves to be priced higher. You have to show higher value to your customers through improvement in quality and the addition of service options and satisfaction guarantees. In many top-of-market brands, they have moved to offer a whole customer experience that goes way beyond just the essential product or service. They have created an experience or a community people are dying to embrace.

I suggest that you start with a 5 percent price increase. As a business owner, you may sweat the change, but most people won't even notice such a small increase in price. Over the next months, you can add extra options and improvements that validate raising the price another 5 to 10 percent. You can introduce a new platinum level to your product or service with a corresponding cost at that level. Over time, by raising value and creating a customer experience with your product or service, you might be able to increase prices by 20 to 40 percent.

Once you change your pricing, you'll notice corresponding changes in your sales performance. When customers begin buying at your higher price, you'll see the light and merit of selling Mercedes-grade products.

Ultimately, every business aspires to be the top name in their industry. This doesn't happen by pricing at the bargain basement. You want your brand to be highly valued by consumers in the marketplace. The key is to build higher quality into your product or service, the kind of value new and experienced repeat customers will appreciate. In the end, value justifies price.

SELL EVERY DAY, NO MATTER WHAT

———

Most business owners remember the early days when they were struggling and would do anything to make a sale. They knocked on doors, made cold calls, and went to trade shows. Some went so far as to dress up as mascots in costumes, standing on street corners with signs just to get customer attention. They did whatever it took to get started.

Later on, when they reach a level of stability and recurring sales, they lose that level of fanatical drive and commitment. The daily focus to sell, sell, sell gets replaced with operational issues, such as staff, delivery, administration, and finances. The original, radical sales efforts they made to get the business off the ground falls by the wayside. Then, when business starts to slow, they can't figure out why sales are falling off.

I asked a highly successful realtor about his secret to long-term success. This is someone who makes in excess of $700,000 annually. He summed it up for me simply, saying that he still makes cold calls every day. He calls until he connects with five new prospects. It can take ten minutes or as many as forty-five, but he sticks to the plan. No matter how many homes he's sold or listed, he remains committed to his daily formula of cold calling to drum up more business. He said that prospecting in this way keeps him sharp and always hungry for more.

He's the exception. Most salespeople, and most companies, work hard on delivery, but make little or no time for fresh sales work. This is why they experience cycles of feast or famine. When a busy delivery cycle ends, they find themselves starting from zero all over again. It's because they forget that ongoing business development is an absolute must.

No matter how busy your company gets, it crucial to keep selling every day to insulate yourself from the downside. Ten minutes a day or just three calls out to people is still better than turning your back on new sales.

To ensure a constant sales flow, commit yourself to creating a company culture that demands ongoing sales productivity. Envision your business as one that expects sales activity daily and embraces innovation with a return to those crazy sales antics that started it all.

COMMIT TO THE LONG SELL

———

Many salespeople tend to work short term from one deal to the next. They focus on the transaction right in front of them and ignore the longer-term opportunities just around the corner. Smart sellers instead play the long game. They're the ones looking around the bend to future orders so they can keep sales ongoing.

The ideal client buys from you all the time. He or she comes back repeatedly to buy more, ask for help, and to find out what else you have on offer. That's the kind of relationship you want to have with your customers. It's the kind of relationship that is maximized by focusing on the long game, not just transactions from one moment to the next.

I advise building a long-term client focus into your sales

process. View your clients not just as the people who buy today, but as the customers who'll be buying all year long. This kind of thinking centers on understanding and knowing them better. What are your customers' needs and wants? What's important in their lives? How can your service or product play a role in making their lives better?

Each customer has a lifetime of value to your company. If someone told you that they'd like to commit to buying regularly for the next ten years, how would you respond? You'd gladly drive to their office or home to serve them. You'd offer far more service and extras than you would to a one-time buyer. You'd look at how you could improve pricing.

Buying and selling is a two-way street. A customer's commitment to your company influences how you treat them. In turn, your long-term commitment to building ongoing customer relationships influences how customers relate to you. They will respond to your interest in them with their own interest in what your company offers. Relationships are good for business—it's a win-win for both parties.

A client of mine was in the business of selling huge compressors for oil field service. The company typically sold one compressor at a time for about $1 million. After they'd make a sale, the team would dance around the office, then start looking to generate the next sale. One of their salespeople, with a little encouragement, decided to change up his selling strategy. He asked a client how many units they expected to buy in the coming year. The client told him they were budgeted for fifteen units. With that very significant piece of information, the salesman asked, "Would you be willing to buy all of those units from us?" The client told him they wouldn't buy all fifteen from one supplier, but could go as high as ten units if they could work a better price for the deal, or get something extra included. It was agreed that they'd cut the price by roughly 10 percent and extend the warranty. They booked a sale for ten units at $9 million. In that one transaction, only two months into their new fiscal year, my client secured an entire year of sales and a predictable cash flow. They accomplished this simply by thinking long term and by changing the questions they asked an existing client.

Effective sales is based on the intention, commitment, and effort to serve clients for the long term. It's like the difference in mindset between planning a date versus planning a marriage—a very different commitment level, right? Clients and prospects appreciate working with sellers who are in it for the long game beyond a single transaction.

SELL THE IDEAL CLIENT

———

Do you ever want to kick yourself for signing a contract with a client who grinds you on price, needs all sorts of hand-holding and extra service, demands an unrealistic timeline, pays late, and then complains about the level of service or the quality of the product? A little voice inside you was screaming, "No, don't do it!" And you did it anyway. Why?

You needed cash flow and sales, and you had to pay your bills. You couldn't see any other way to do it, so you bit the bullet and signed the client, even though you knew that subpar clients are 80 percent of your client troubles.

The key to avoiding subpar clients is learning how to reach the multitude of ideal clients who are out there. Only then will you be able to give up the desperate pull to work with any warm body who will buy.

The first step is to clearly define your ideal client:

- What are they like?
    - Easy to work with and open to ideas
- How do they do business?
    - Fast to pay, open to change, and good at making decisions
- What's their demographic?
    - Female, thirty-five to fifty years old, college-educated, active professional, who is active on social media and is wanting to find a new way to work out outside of a traditional gym (The demographic will change based on the business.)

Your ability to define the traits of your ideal client is critical to your success. The first two questions and answers would apply to any ideal client. The third question about demographics will change, of course, with the particulars of your product or service.

Work with your team to define your ideal customer avatar. Your salespeople should be able to zero in on the kind of personal and professional traits that characterize the kind of clients they enjoy working with.

The next step is to figure out where to find your ideal clients. Where do they work? Where do they live? Where do they play? Who do they socialize with? What's their key issue that you can solve? Too often we act like these people are four-leaf clovers, but for most businesses the ideal client is plentiful. In today's global market, four-leaf clovers are everywhere!

After you know where to find them, you need to figure out how to attract them. Are you the ideal solution for your ideal client?

I worked with a hardwood supplier and installer who defined his ideal client as major home builders with large projects in multiple cities. He knew how to find these potential clients through national builders' associations. But when I asked him, "Why would these major home builders buy from you?" his answer was a long, pained silence.

Finally, he said, "Well, I guess because we're cheaper."

I explained that no home builder became a national company just by choosing the cheapest option available. "What else can you offer?" I asked.

His reply was, "I don't know."

We spent six weeks working out the details of how his product and delivery needed to change. He had to ensure that major home builders would see the benefits of working with his company. He decided to expand his line of exotic woods and put installation guarantees in place. He also decided to include travel in his pricing and daily cleanup as part of the installation process. These changes in product line and service made his company highly attractive to his ideal client, and ultimately brought in the business and contracts he was looking for.

You can do the same. Once you identify and know where to find your ideal client, you can make the changes you need to attract them to doing business with you. When you have those pieces in place, you'll no longer need to make deals with subpar clients who don't add up to success.

PART FOUR

MARKETING: THE UNICORN OF BUSINESS

I ran an advertising and marketing agency for five years. It was a fantastic experience in some ways and terrible in others. By the time I decided to leave the business, I hated everything about it. Actually, though, I love marketing. I just hate how the business of marketing usually plays out.

What I discovered during my years in the marketing industry is that a significant percentage of marketing professionals know very little about how to do it well. Even when they get results, they don't know why. More often they don't get results, and they still don't know why. They confuse good design with good strategy. They confuse "likes" and "clicks" with effective business results.

I learned that few people in the business of marketing knew how to think strategically. In the end, I realized that a marketing agency that can strategize, execute, and get real results is a marketing unicorn—very rare and hard to find.

Yet I still have hope. I believe that marketing is essential for every business to grow and spread awareness of its brand. It's the critical tool to leverage strong sales and take your business to the next level.

Marketing has a farther reach than sales and personal contacts in the marketplace. Good marketing can fill your inbox with orders and get your phone ringing with inquiries. When done right, marketing can induce buying decisions on your Facebook page or Instagram account. It's difficult for companies to grow without constant, effective marketing campaigns. Successful companies plan, execute, measure, and adapt their marketing constantly.

The key to effective marketing is to run it with the same accountability of performance as other areas of your business, such as sales, production, and finance. Marketing also opens the door to a creative and fun process that can get the results you need to expand your company's reach.

BRAND AWARENESS WILL BE THE DEATH OF YOU

———

Brand awareness is the holy grail of marketing. But if I hear one more marketing guru try to sell small- and medium-sized business owners on some global marketing scheme to build their "brand awareness," I might just injure someone!

Coca-Cola can spend millions online, on TV, and in magazines, stores, and sports arenas to hold their coveted place in the minds of consumers. They can spend multi-millions on messaging awareness of their brand so that when you're thirsty, you reach for a Coke. But it won't work for a company that has a marketing budget of thousands, not millions.

Smaller businesses just can't buy that volume of exposure in enough places and enough of the time to own a brand spot in every consumer's mind. At the advertising agency I owned, we had a guy on staff who'd played a role in the original Intel Inside campaign. A small software company came to see him about starting a marketing campaign just like Intel's. He had to break it to them that a campaign of that kind would cost a cool $100 million. That sobered them up pretty quickly to choose a more practical and affordable approach.

The practical approach is called "direct-response marketing," which emphasizes moving people to act. Direct-response marketing is less about big marketing campaigns, and more about making an offer to consumers so they are motivated to respond with a time-sensitive action.

For example, we wanted to try direct mail for our restaurants, but knew that typical flyers didn't work. So, we designed a mailing that looked like a wedding invitation. On the front it said, "You're Invited," and when people opened the envelope it offered them a complimentary bottle of wine when they came in and dined with us. Each night we counted the number of responses and added their email addresses to our database. In this way we could eventually send them promos electronically and save the mailing costs. We had great returns on this promotion, which was about eight times as effective as most unaddressed ad mail. Direct-response marketing is more about engaging people, than flashing a brand in their face.

In the restaurant business, I also learned that brand awareness, even when it works, is often useless. People were always telling me that they'd heard about my restaurants, yet they'd never eaten at one. Brand awareness had basically zero effect on our business and sales. It was just good intentions, but all the good intentions in the world mean nothing if people don't take action. Action is what drives sales and response. Action is the result of effective, measured, direct-response marketing.

We had a client who provided cleanup services for industrial sites. The business mailed brochures to target customers multiple times with zero response. Their biggest issue was that customers only called when they had an industrial spill or accident, and no one could foresee when that would be. Direct-response marketing has to be creative in its appeal and has to stick in the potential customer's memory. Since the client knew who they wanted to target, we could spend more on the marketing package.

One of our genius staff came up with an idea for an Office Spill Kit designed for small spills that could be placed on an office shelf or in a lunchroom. The kit was substantial enough in perceived value that people were unlikely to throw it away. It contained everything needed for office spills, including soda water, bleach pens, a new white shirt, and it was branded with the cleanup company's name. People thought it was cute and handy, and it created goodwill. Two weeks later, the first call came in about an industrial spill. When the spill occurred, the kit was there with our client's phone number and the message, "Call Now!"

When it comes to marketing, you need to be thinking about measuring response. This is where digital marketing is infinitely effective for tracking people's responses and actions, and it can be automated. For instance, a good Facebook marketing campaign can A/B test every headline, image, and word in an online ad. You never know what combination will work best to create clicks and cause people to take action. You can test for next to no money before you broadly launch your campaigns. With cookies on a web page, you can track the initial clicks and follow people all over the web.

At the face-to-face, in-person level, you need to be asking every person who crosses the threshold of your business how they heard about you. Unfortunately, people often don't accurately recall how they heard about your business. A bakery eliminated this issue by having teenage kids hand out coupons for a free cinnamon bun when customers came in the shop. Every coupon came with a specific code that could be tracked to a specific date, location, and teenager. Oh, and people always bought more than one cinnamon bun. This clever form of marketing was a revenue-generating activity that made them money.

Before you say yes to any form of marketing, establish how you will measure response. Even digital marketing can be done wrong and not require people to take action, so be wary. Look beyond brand awareness in your marketing to actually bring people into the store, showroom, or website for a purchase.

Direct-response marketing done well is *the* way to build brand awareness.

KNOW YOUR ROMI

I entered the marketing industry in 2010 as an interim CEO tasked with turning an advertising agency around. I thought that a good deliverable for our clients, and a key differentiator for our business, would be the results of our clients' marketing campaigns.

I was quickly "set straight" by one of our longtime ad men who told me that "results are too hard to control. We just do the work, push it out into the market, and hope it flies." That's the traditional thinking in the industry. They are interested in the art of advertising and the process of marketing, but they aren't really concerned with results.

Of course, there are companies and marketing people who are striving to make every campaign work for their clients. It's the client's job to seek out those agencies and invest their marketing dollars wisely.

Any business owner who invests in marketing wants to see a reasonable "return on marketing investment" (ROMI) for the money they spend. To calculate this, first you subtract out the costs of marketing and then you divide by the costs of marketing. For example, if an Instagram campaign costs $2,200 and generates $30,000 in revenue then the formula is [$30,000–$2,200]/$2,200. The result can be expressed as a percent, but often we express the result in dollars. "For every dollar spent we generated $12 in revenue."

Every business with a marketing budget needs to be monitoring, calculating, and improving their return on marketing investment. With the advent of digital marketing, ROMI is far easier to measure.

For example, a large retail client that sold fitness products was spending almost $100,000 a month in online advertising. They (with the help of my friend Dave) tracked the activity of every web page, each Google ad, and monitored every click to correlate who actually bought on their website. It took almost a full-time person to simply track, refine, and administer the online campaign. When their equipment supplier decided to take over the online advertising, they increased the budget by three times to over $300,000 a month. They got fewer clicks and sales, and worse results. Why? Because the supplier simply threw money at every online ad, platform, and keyword without taking the time to measure the components of their online promotion. They didn't know which tactics were effective and which weren't, and so their costs skyrocketed, leaving them scratching their heads.

With traditional marketing methods, such as direct mail, you can still calculate ROMI; it just takes a little more creativity to track the mailing and the response of your prospects. Typically a traditional marketing campaign needs to have something redeemed, something brought in, or some code entered. Clients often say that people won't bring this mailing in. However, with a strong enough offer, people will, and do. The complimentary bottle of wine mentioned in Secret 31 proves this to be true several thousand times over.

One of the best keys to remember here is to give something for free. In a direct-response mail promotion, a tire shop offered a free car air freshener and 15 percent off on the customer's next tire order. The mail piece was a cutout that looked like one of those air freshener pine trees that hang on a rearview mirror. Every day they couldn't believe the number of people who came in for a free air freshener and *then* asked about the tire promotion.

As a business owner, I've dealt with many advertising sales representatives who are single-mindedly driven to book the sale. I've also dealt with creative departments and people who are driven by the inspiration of creation. Finding marketing agencies that can effectively build a creative campaign *and* effectively measure it can be difficult.

When shopping around for a marketing partner, be sure to inquire about the software they use to track results. Ask them three questions:

1. How often do they provide reporting on the results internally, and to you, the client?
2. What changes or adaptations do they make to campaigns if they aren't performing well?
3. Do they have a target conversion rate or a click-through rate on every piece of a campaign? (They should.)

Once you commit to measuring your marketing spends and advertising efforts, you quickly start to determine which tactics and methods work best for your business. Marketing strategies aren't the same for every industry or company. There is a period of testing, measuring, and experimenting. Commit to your marketing, but be vigilant in measuring ROMI and the marketing partner you've chosen to work with.

STOP WASTING YOUR MONEY

When business leaders ask me what's the best way to reduce their marketing budget, I tell them, "STOP! Stop all the advertising and marketing that isn't working."

I'll tell you the same thing: Put the brakes on your marketing budget. Then, one by one, try each marketing method for a period of time and measure it individually to see what effect it has on traffic, inquiries, and sales. This pragmatic approach to testing each marketing tactic will let you know what actually works. Most companies come to the ugly realization that most of their marketing is generating poor results.

As the saying goes, "Half my marketing is working, I just don't know which half."

One of my clients was a local home builder who was spending $86,000 a year on magazine advertising that couldn't be adequately tracked for its effectiveness. He had no idea whether or not those ads were driving potential buyers to see his show homes. I suggested that he stop the magazine advertising for two months, and lo and behold, the customer traffic to his sales centers didn't change. We then spent $1,400 on A-frame signs placed within blocks of his sales center to capitalize on street traffic. The result was a 16 to 18 percent improvement in visits to his show homes. He saved more than $84,000 that went directly into his pocket and his bottom line.

A year later, he started running the magazine ads again. When I asked him why, he told me that he liked seeing the ads, and friends always complimented him about them, saying they looked great. It was a case of marketing for his own ego. It happens all the time. Business owners love to see their logo and name in lights. This doesn't mean it's effective, but it may be. If you want to do it, just be honest with yourself about why. Better yet, find out what really works, put your money where it gets the most pragmatic results, and *then* enjoy seeing your business in advertising.

KNOW YOUR TRIBE

———

Do you know your tribe of existing customers? What are your customers' interests, their tastes in food, music, and fashion? Where do they live? Where do they shop? Does your current tribe of customers align with your ideal prospects? Most companies haven't taken the time to get to know their customers or to build customer profiles into a company database. They haven't yet learned how to personalize their customer experience.

Customers who are attracted to a particular company's brand share traits with others who are attracted to the same brand. It's like speaking the same language and sharing the same cultural symbols, whether it's Apple computers or Harley-Davidson motorcycles. When you know your tribe's language, you can speak their voice in your marketing, in your messaging, and on social media. It's the voice your tribe trusts and responds to. It's the voice that has them thinking and feeling, "This company really gets me!"

Who is your ideal customer? Who's in your tribe? Company owners often tell me that "everyone" is in their tribe. What they don't get is that everyone is not a tribe. Remember, tribes speak the same "language" and have similar cultural traits. I tell owners to think of their very best customer and then to describe that customer in great detail.

Define your customer avatar, your very best tribe member. Define them with thirty different characteristics. Their social circle, their hobbies, their physical attributes, their education, websites they visit. You get the idea. Now you have a solid tribe member profile.

Everything about your business needs to focus on and cater to your tribe, starting with your products and marketing. Marketing should reach out to the tribe and depict your tribe members. Messaging should speak to their issues, inform them, and clue into what makes them tick; what's most important to them. Your products and services should meet the needs of your tribe. Your guarantee should reassure them.

Businesses spend too much time, effort, and money hiring third-party marketing "experts" who craft clever messages and taglines without ever knowing or truly understanding their client tribe and ideal customer. Instead, a company's marketing should first involve defining its tribe and knowing everything about them. When you make this your starting point, your messaging will speak to your tribe and resonate with them. This is how you build a brand and a tribe of loyal customers.

TEN-LEGGED TABLE

———

Marketing is becoming more of a science. With the pro-liferation of digital marketing tools tracking every click, view, and result, marketing has entered an age of highly sophisticated metrics. Yet the predictive success of a spe-cific ad or marketing piece is still very challenging.

Marketing campaigns are designed with good intent, solid judgment, and some basis for assuming good results to come. In the abstract "bubble" of a marketing test group, the campaign is often a winner. Then it goes live and gets tested in the real world. Some of the marketing campaigns I was convinced were going to fail actually did very well. Others that I thought would be rockstar performers wound up crashing and burning.

The solution to reaching your ideal customer and tribe involves creating, producing, and using multiple mar-keting tools, platforms, and messages. A good marketing program, regardless of size, uses a wide variety of marketing tools that can be measured and evaluated for performance. Marketing is a grand, ongoing experiment in consistent, measurable results.

Start to build your "marketing table" with ten, rather than four legs. Then follow your metrics to whittle those legs down to the primary four to six that work best. In our hyper-fast marketplace where competition for attention and interest of audiences is fierce, you need to try new strategies and marketing platforms, constantly innovating to perform at the highest level. With your ten-legged marketing table, you keep experimenting with new marketing tools to gain a deeper understanding and measurable results. All while the proven tools keep running.

Over time you'll see which marketing legs keep your table standing and which provide no visible support. As you experiment you'll be left with three or four ultra-effective marketing tools that you know are working consistently and bringing the results you need. These are your keepers, even as you continue innovating, and always improving the design of your marketing table.

SECRET 36

DON'T BE A PIONEER

___

It's awesome to tell other business owners that you're using the latest social media platform as part of your marketing mix: "Snapchat is killing it for us these days!" Or that you're focusing on a new digital publishing platform that's saving time and money. It's great to be on the cutting edge of marketing innovation.

Unfortunately, many of the latest marketing tools are pioneer territory, which isn't where you want to be. Some may hold promise as new spaces in which to connect with your target tribe, but many can be costly in both time and money. You can spend months, even years, learning and measuring the content cost of a new platform or digital funnel, testing the effectiveness of each new ad design. You might get lucky and have a breakthrough that gets incredible results. For most business owners, however, it's a pipe dream. We just don't have the time, money, or energy to be pioneering new marketing tools.

The people selling new platforms and marketing concepts are absolutely convinced they've struck marketing gold. But before committing to the latest innovation, ask for specific results, case studies, and examples that mirror your business. Every new platform has a "Google story" of a company that used it and became the "global dominator in their field." Every new marketing tool will boast about a company that used it and killed it in their industry; but did that Google story occur in your city, your industry, and your market? Probably not.

Rather than taking pioneering leaps with newly minted marketing tools, make sure to review demonstrable results that match and mirror your business. Be sure to reach out to companies that have succeeded with the new tool in controlled campaigns. Then, and only then, should you consider using it. Remember, pioneering has always been dangerous work with big risks and little payback.

RULE OF THREE

If you've ever been to a trade show, you've walked past hundreds, maybe thousands of booths, from size 10x10 to giant 30x10 spreads. They range from basic folding tables staffed by one to 3-D castles with lights, moving parts, and sound effects.

All trade shows follow the Rule of Three: it takes three seconds to decide whether or not a display gets your attention.

The next time you walk along the carpeted path of a trade show, see how long it takes you to decide whether or not to stop at a booth or display. The question, "Is this interesting to me?" takes three seconds to answer, not ten or twenty. That's how challenging it is for trade show participants to initially connect with individuals in a crowded space—all they get is three seconds.

The key to marketing at trade shows, or in any other context, is the immediate impact of your messaging, your visuals, and ads. You have three seconds to have an impact with a message that touches, shocks, or emotionally moves people. An image, logo, tagline, or headline shouldn't take more than three seconds for a person to understand, digest, and feel the impact. If it takes longer than that, your potential customer has already passed you by.

I use the Rule of Three for new marketing material. I'll show an ad or message, like showing a flashcard, and simply ask, "What's this about? Are you interested?" People's answers and facial expressions are a sure tell of whether a marketing piece is engaging enough to be effective in three seconds. It happens so fast that people can't fake their response. Either the marketing message elicits an immediate emotional or intellectual reaction, or it doesn't. It either hits or it misses.

If you're successful in your first three seconds, it buys you another ten. The initial interest generates thought. People stop for more, another ten seconds to see what the product offers. It's like reading a headline in a newspaper or online and deciding to read a little bit more. You continue to the first paragraph or scan the first few subheadings. You spend about thirteen seconds in all before deciding to read further.

If your marketing is successful at the thirteen-second mark, you've earned the person's attention for another thirty seconds. This is why it's so important for your messaging to follow the increments of three seconds, ten seconds, and thirty seconds. Each increment of time should increase your audience's interest.

Sales operates the same way. In sales you provide a solid question or statement in the first three seconds that's tantalizing enough to hold a potential buyer for the next ten seconds of explanation. If the buyer is still interested, you've earned another thirty seconds to elaborate on your pitch. If the product and pitch are really interesting, a potential buyer will commit to another three minutes. If they are even more interested, they'll up their ante to a thirty-minute meeting or discussion.

Try experimenting with the Rule of Three on anyone who isn't a coworker or involved in the marketing project. See how it works to determine whether or not a marketing message is effective enough at increments of three, ten, and thirty seconds, then three minutes. If it really goes well, you'll know you have an effective ad, message, or display.

60 MILES AN HOUR

———

How come so many people in marketing don't understand the average speed of a car? At 60 mph, a driver can only take in so much of a billboard. If it catches your eye with the words "World's Best Sandwich" that's enough to arrest your attention. All you need to know then is the restaurant name and the exit number. There isn't time to read about the artisan bread or homemade cheese. All you need to know is there's a great sandwich further up the road.

You'd think that more marketing professionals would understand that simple and clear messages are the most compelling. That's what to strive for in marketing your business. You need to get people's attention with as few words as possible. Once you nail it with your message, you're halfway to a sale.

Whether your message is on a billboard, a web page, or

a sandwich board outside your place of business, you need a crisp and effective headline to grab the customer: "Energy in a Bottle!" What follows is another short sub-head that signals a call to action: "Subscribe Now!"

In today's marketing world, brevity is the key to good messaging and quick response. The 60 mph billboard reads "World's Best Sandwich" with a killer picture, "On your right in 150 yards." Website travel moves at more like 30 mph, but you still need to bring the customer in quickly. You can add a sentence or two of details, even a short, high-interest video with quality images to entice more interest. Your goal is to hold interest just long enough to compel the customer to take action. With that, your marketing message has done its job.

Stop thinking in terms of whole sentences to convey your message. Stop trying to find more descriptive words. Start thinking in terms of three to seven simple words that sum it up. At 60 mph, you have to pull me into your product or service FAST.

PAY FOR THE THINKING, SHOP FOR THE DELIVERY

———

Do you know why most marketing sucks? It's because not enough thinking and strategizing went into it. Many of the people in marketing are doers who execute basic tactics within a strategy, but that's the easy part. There are plenty of people who can do that. The hard part is finding a marketing professional who can really brainstorm, strategize, and deliver what will work for your size and profile of business.

You can get a cookie-cutter logo for $5 on a site like Fiverr. Or you can pay $200 to have designers compete for your business on 99Designs. But how much thinking and strategizing will go into that design?

Many clients and friends come to me with some new marketing plan they've been sold on. I review the plan and think, "this is terrible." It either doesn't fit the person's business or it isn't focused on the results they want.

So how can a business owner sift through all the marketing speak and hard sell to know if what they're getting is solid and worthwhile? Here are some points I keep in mind when evaluating whether someone is giving me good marketing strategy:

- When I ask them to explain my business back to me, they can do it with ease. That's when I know they truly get what I do.
- Is the marketing measurable? Can we assign values to it and watch for results?
- Do they have a solid grasp of strategy, as opposed to particular tactics, such as ad buys? A broader strategy can be applied to many tactical delivery tools.
- Does the recommended strategy generate excitement and interest in you?
- Does the strategy build like a good play or movie with layers of design, script, and characters? Is it planned in stages of tactics that build on one another? Remember, the whole is greater than the sum of its parts.
- Is there a timeline to execute, a defined outcome, and a sales target? Good strategy has corners and parameters.
- Can they show you other case studies that demonstrate a problem, how they crafted the strategy, why it worked, and the actual results?

- Most people in marketing offer solutions based on what they sell. A marketing firm that builds websites believes every prospect needs a new website or an update. They don't consider whether or not it's the best thing for you at this time. Beware of the hammer salesman who calls everything a nail. It also pays to have a healthy skepticism of marketers (at least in the beginning).

Take your time, question the proposed strategy, and see how it measures up to the questions listed. Don't be afraid to pay top dollar for a strategy that will take your marketing and promotion to the next level. It can be one of the best investments you make.

THE DIGITAL HORSE WINS BY A NOSE

There is no single marketing strategy that is absolutely better than any other. There is no single marketing tactic that is universally the best. Anything from old-school direct mail to online Instagram campaigns or Facebook ads can be effective marketing solutions. It all depends on the context: the product, the service, the targeted audience, the marketplace, and many other variables.

Yet, all things considered, in today's global marketplace the winner by a nose is digital marketing. There, I said it—and I mean it. Digital marketing has many advantages over traditional marketing tools and should be the initial and primary focus of your marketing efforts.

Here's why:

- Digital is more measurable for actions taken, volume of activity, clicks, and views.
- It is more cost-effective on a per-prospect-reached basis.
- You can tag or "pixel" visitors to your website and follow their activity online. (What? You didn't know you've been pixeled?!)
- You can target prospects based on anything and everything from age to location, occupation, and interests.
- You can reach people 24/7 wherever they are through their smartphones.
- Responses can be instantaneous and easy as the tap of a screen.
- You can gather marketing information about a prospect by leveraging their online profiles, buying habits, and posted content.
- You can turn a campaign on or off in an instant, whether because it's not working or because it's generating too much business (as if there is ever such a thing!)

There you have it in a nutshell. Digital marketing is more effective than traditional marketing. I've experienced it at my own companies where I've found the management and measurement of digital marketing far easier and more efficient, delivering the best results long term.

However, digital marketing is an ever-changing and

sometimes daunting challenge. You need to be prepared to dive into a steep learning curve of digital material and processes. Once you make the leap, you'll be way ahead of your competition. Yet, few business owners are equipped to take on digital marketing all by themselves. You'll likely need to hire someone already skilled in the digital universe whom you can trust to maximize the digital space for your business.

In summation, digital marketing wins the race, right? Yes, but not always. For example, when I opened a new restaurant, we used digital marketing to target people in the area. We did text campaigns, AdWords, and Facebook advertising with many variations of content, all with limited effectiveness for driving people to the restaurant. Then we went old school with direct mail and included a discount coupon people could bring with them to the restaurant. The cost was ten times our digital marketing, but it got us more than fourteen times the response.

That experience goes to show that the best marketing is the kind that gets the best measurable and predictable results. You won't know for sure until you break from the gate and test the track. Experience will tell, but my money is still on the digital horse to win the steeplechase by a nose.

PART FIVE

—

BUSINESS IS PEOPLE

Your balance sheet goes home at night. I love that expression, though it's a little hard to understand at first. Your balance sheet is a snapshot of the financial condition of your company. Contrary to popular belief, however, the best indicator of your company's financial position isn't its assets, liabilities, and net worth, but its people. They are the ones who go home at night, and people are the life-breath of any company.

I used to pay lip service to how important people are to a business. I understood that people are important, but I really didn't think they were THE most important component of a business' success. I figured cash, products, sales, good marketing, and other fiscal components ranked higher to a business than its people. I was wrong.

My good friend Ben is one of the best salespeople I've ever met. He can read sales situations like a Jedi. He has owned construction companies, and has sold real estate, software, and major infrastructure engineering. As wise as he is, when we first met I thought he was clueless because he didn't understand the technical aspects of the software we were selling. Yet he sold better than anyone. When I asked him how he was so effective, he told me, "Marty, it's all about the people. The features and all the technical stuff doesn't matter." He'd say it often, like a mantra, "Marty, business *is* people." I thought I understood what he meant, but for a long time I just got it on the surface level. Sure, a business can't run without people, that's not hard to understand. But Ben was persistent, and eventually I began to comprehend the depth of what he meant. Gradually I came to notice the many business situations wherein the most important factor determining success is the people.

I looked at companies where financial performance and brand satisfaction were strong, and I saw how these results were generated by above-average people working on above-average teams. It brought me to an understanding that the number one job of a business owner is to staff the organization with outstanding people.

When you invest time and energy in your people, that commitment is reflected in sales and market share. If you treat your staff like the most important part of your business, they will go the extra mile to deliver superior performance. A smart owner will help staff advance their careers, and let them know they are appreciated for their hard work and dedication. The best way to build your company is by building teams of talented, committed, and responsible staff who care about each other, the company, and everyone's mutual success.

Long after you sell your company or shut it down and move onto other challenges, you'll have the relationships you created with the people you hired, trained, and worked alongside. A contented, dedicated staff will be reflected in satisfied customers, because when it's all said and done, business *is* people.

SOLVE THE PROBLEM

—

I hate it when people say they tried, but failed to fix a business problem. "I tried" doesn't come with a consolation prize. Customers don't care about trying, they need problems fixed. "Try" is not a solution. It's an excuse people use to justify the fact that they didn't get it done. "Trying" only pushes the problem back on the team or back on the boss. Someone that settles for "trying" in your company is just sweeping problems off their desk. The biggest failures in business ultimately come down to the inability to solve problems.

Staff who "try," but fail to provide actionable solutions, also tend to offer weak apologies that are even more infuriating. Offering a half-hearted apology to disguise a weak effort only adds insult to injury.

Company owners need to bang the drum of "solve the problem" so that staff know it's important to their success at your company. This needs to be a foundation of the way your organization works. Commit to a company culture that is clear about this: At company XYZ, we *do*, we don't *try*. One way or another we find, create, or innovate solutions.

There are two major reasons why an employee will hide behind making a sad attempt without really committing to solving a problem:

1. They perceive that "trying" to solve the problem, even if it's a feeble or ineffective attempt, is safer than doing nothing. Job safety is their only motivating factor.
2. They are not really empowered or educated to solve the problem. The team member recognizes the issue and understands it, but isn't really empowered by their level of authority to solve it. They actually have never been trained on the approved recourse for the problem.

These issues are exemplified by a recent hotel experience when I was kept awake most of the night by a group partying in the next room. Upon checkout when the staff asked me how my stay was, I gave them a rundown of the noise and lack of response from the night staff. The front desk clerk said, "Oh, sorry to hear that," but there was no effort to make amends.

I pressed, "Is there something you can do to make good on this?"

The clerk said, "Well, let me find out." He went through a door, then came back saying that he wanted to comp my room charges, but he wasn't able to find the supervisor. He said he wasn't sure about how to enter it into the computer system. I pressed him further, and he admitted that he wasn't authorized to activate the solution. The fact remains that anyone working at that front desk needed to have the authorization.

Business owners need to empower their teams to solve problems on the spot when they occur. They should expect and require staff to think on their feet to meet customer needs. Even when a solution isn't ideal, staff should be commended for making a decision to take action. Alternative solutions can be discussed and improvements made so that staff are empowered to offer a better solution the next time.

We live in a society where problem-solving is no longer the expectation. Don't be surprised when your new hires aren't naturally equipped with this skillset. Problem-solving has to be developed and trained via onboarding programs that teach staff problem-solving tools that work for your company.

Successful problem-solving also should be recognized

regularly and celebrated among management and staff. Recognition and reward ensure that problem-solving grows as an integral part of your company culture and standard business practices.

CULTURE—IT'S NOT JUST FOR EUROPEANS

———

Company culture is one of those things that people in business love to talk about. It's trendy and everyone touts it as a key to business success, yet few companies know how to actively use company culture day-to-day. It's often just a passive concept. Most companies get the management team together for a one-day workshop to create a culture statement. It goes into the employee binder and onto a wall plaque in the reception area, then no one ever thinks about it again. Many companies don't have a method or process for bringing their company culture into their business practices.

Here are the keys to creating a winning company culture:

1. Defined by the Group: The most effective cultures are developed and refined by the people in the orga-

nization themselves. A company culture isn't some boilerplate list of values that's simply handed down from the president's desk. A meaningful company culture represents core beliefs that everyone actively buys into and adopts in their daily work. It helps breathe life and purpose into company operations.

2. Five Words: A great company culture can be summarized in five words. Why five? Because anything more than five words is difficult for staff, customers, and suppliers to remember. Three or four words is even better, but five words forces an organization to focus on the most critical core values and beliefs that will motivate the whole group, and not be forgotten.

3. Shared Definition: Each of those five words must have a clear definition and meaning, easily understood and shared by everyone on staff. When we made "family" a key word at my company, I discovered that there were many different perceptions and connotations of the word. It's the same with loyalty, honesty, and service. Everyone has different interpretations depending on their own experiences. Therefore, each word needs to have a clearly crafted definition that is universally understood by everyone in your business.

4. Actively Managed: Business owners are famous for saying, "We don't really have a culture here." But the fact is, they do. It's just being actively created by the worst employee at the company. Culture is alive and organic, and unless it is responsibly created and

managed, encouraged and discussed, the void will be filled by what is easiest and laziest to say or do. Great company culture is intentional and idealistic. It needs to be managed and supported daily to provide ideal experiences for customers and staff.

5. Repeated like a Tibetan Monk: You know your company culture is effective when it's on the lips of staff like a mantra on the lips of a Tibetan monk. Some people on staff might express it in ways that sound like, "I know, I know, we always treat our clients like our favorite grandparent or rock star." They might repeat it like a disgruntled twelve-year-old in a mocking Homer Simpson voice, but that proves that they know it by heart. Knowing it is the first step to owning it, and then to living it daily.

8+ CULTURE

———

In my work as an advisor for businesses, I've found that owners, managers, and team leaders are adept at assessing a staff member's job performance in only a matter of seconds. So why do we do 360-degree reviews that take a month and involve six to twelve people to reach a conclusion?

If you're a giant company, you can afford to spend lots of time and money on employee reviews to mitigate risk, provide HR documentation, and give detailed feedback. But as a business owner you don't have the resources for all of that. Out of necessity, you need a system that is fast and simple. That's why I created the 8+ Culture scoring system to help clients evaluate, assess, and measure staff performance quickly and efficiently. It's a straightforward system based on a simple scale of 1 to 10.

It works because our brains are adapted to take in and

process many factors that move us to thousands of different microdecisions daily. We can accurately evaluate people we work with, score them appropriately, and articulate the reasons for that score almost instantaneously.

"Joe is performing at a 7."

"Judy is performing at 8.5 this week!"

8+ Culture scoring is guided by basic parameters that can be summed up as follows, starting with the topmost score:

Score of 10: You're outstanding, don't change a thing. We'd like you to stay and advance your career with us long term.

Score of 8 or 9: You're excellent. There are only a few minor areas we'd like you to focus on and strive to improve, but overall, you're a keeper.

Score of 6 or 7: You're good. There are some areas in your performance that you need to work on. We want you on the team, but need to see some improvement in significant areas that could affect your ability to advance here long term.

Score of 5 or below: You're fired. (This score warrants firing because poor performers will bring down the scores of others around them.)

When and how should you use 8+ scoring? Follow these simple steps:

- For starters, get together with your team leaders at the end of a week, and simply ask each of them to rate their own performance on the 8+ scale. Absolutely, rate your own as well. This practice session gets people thinking about regular evaluations, as they begin to learn the 8+ Culture scoring system. Remember, this is just an exercise, not a binding review. You are beginning the learning process. Openly discuss the scoring and how people arrived at their scores without judgment.
- The next step is for management to start evaluating staff members. Do the managers agree that Joe is a 7 and Judy is an 8.5 this week? Does anyone score a 5 or below? If managers agree that someone is a 4, discuss why and compare opinions. Can the person improve? Are they a mismatch for the company? Is it time to let them go? (Probably).
- Next, begin to apply the 8+ Culture standard to hiring. Evaluate applicants by weighing the overall impression of their resumes, professional experience, and job interviews against the 8+ system. Aim high by hiring only the people who appear to be 8+ performers. You may not always get it right, but at least you have a standard and framework against which to measure applicants.

- Talk with staff about how using 8+ Culture can become a component of your company's overall culture. People will come to understand that superior performance is an essential part of your business model.

Everyone has weeks that are below 8, including you. Make it clear to your team that what you're looking for is an overall performance average. You don't fire someone for having a week when they were distracted, made mistakes, or lacked focus. Let your staff know that performance can vary, and what counts is a person's long-term performance over time. The best way to demonstrate this is to share your own below-par scores, as well as your commitment to measuring up to your own best performance.

8+ Culture is a system for building a positive, transparent culture. It's not a heavy-handed tool. It lets people know that the ideal is to always hire right, help people improve, and keep them long term. Over time, 8+ Culture will become integral to building awareness about high performance at your company.

HIRE ONLY A-PLAYERS

———

Intellectually, you and I both know that we don't want to hire people who are subpar or who aren't ideal for the job. So why are there so many low-performing employees at work today? It's because our best thinking and decision-making are undermined by the urgency of "I need another set of hands today! We can't wait for Mr. or Ms. Right to come along." Too many hiring decisions are made for emotional reasons that override the objective needs of a company. The result is that businesses fail to hire killer team members.

My practical advice and definitive opinion on hiring "someone just to do the job" is this: Don't do it. Don't say yes to the person you know is not the right match for your company. Find another way to make ends meet before you hire subpar people. Pay your other staff overtime, give them bonuses for extra hours, use family you can trust, work the extra time yourself, hire a temp, do anything other than hire the wrong person.

Filling positions with the wrong people comes with added costs to your company. Subpar hires can inflict damage or slow down the work of other good staff. They can destroy morale and undermine the company culture you've worked so hard to create and drill into your team. High performers become frustrated with coworkers who aren't performing at the company's standard of excellence.

Making a hire based on giving someone a chance to improve on the job is a fool's errand. It's a 50/50 proposition at best that training sessions, mentoring, and guidance will bring a subpar hire around to the company's needed level of performance. It doesn't help the person hired or their coworkers to set up a new employee to fail. It can take months of coaching, hoping the new hire will finally "get it." Spare yourself and your team the trouble by only hiring people with the skillset and work ethic the position requires.

Sometimes a C-level player you hire is great, though not at their job. For instance, I once hired a guy who was the life of the party, a fantastic person to have a beer with. Mike wowed us with his English accent, bad sweaters, and other fashion blunders. Everyone liked him, but he was a dismal failure at his job. He missed every deadline, got basic instructions wrong, and had others redo his work regularly. I finally had to fire Mike for incompetence, but I told him he could remain part of our "alumni" and attend our social functions. He was thrilled and so was the team. Moral of the story: you can make friends with incompetent people, but don't invite them into your business.

Always strive to find A-players you can believe in with both your head *and* your gut. Don't let stressful times or situations pressure you into hiring the wrong person. It's far better to find a temporary remedy while you search for the right person for the job. Maintain the integrity of your team by always taking the time necessary to fill positions with A-players who will meet the needs of your company.

BATTERIES INCLUDED

Your business is not an educational institution or apprenticeship program for students looking to learn new skills. It's a for-profit business that strives every day to reach peak performance. The people you bring into the company need to come equipped on day one with the talent and skills to perform at a high level.

You can't afford to staff your company with people who need on-the-job training. You need to hire people who will hit the ground running the first week, not some intern who needs to "get up to speed" over the course of six to nine months. Small to midsized companies don't have the cash and resources to spend on training programs, apprenticeships, and academies. The costs are too great in salaries and lost productivity. For the average business, it's too big a cost for a limited reward.

Dan Sullivan of Strategic Coach uses the phrase "batteries included" to mean that employees need to show up with the energy, attitude, basic skills, and knowledge to contribute to your business from the moment you hire them. You need to fully stock your company with outstanding staff before you can begin to create a feeder system for newbies.

Only when you are fully staffed with exceptional staff in place can you entertain the idea of bringing in trainees to learn the ropes. Until then, hire people who are self-starters, fully equipped with batteries included to excel at their new jobs. It's the only way to effectively grow your business without delay.

HOW COMMITTED IS YOUR STAFF?

———

If I had a dollar for every entrepreneur who expressed frustration that their staff weren't as committed to their business as they were, I'd be retired a few times over on some private island in Fiji. Your employees might really love their work, but your business is rarely their primary goal and passion. They simply aren't as invested in the company as you are.

You've risked capital, family finances, and your former career to launch a business. You've followed a burning passion and committed everything to create a successful, growing company. You are in neck deep, with no backup plan. You desperately need your venture to work. At best, your team members really love their jobs, but they're not hanging on your company's success the way you are. See the difference?

You can inspire commitment in your team, but only up to a point. You can inspire pride and belief in your company's vision and goals. Staff members will support your culture and even advocate for your business, but please don't expect them to give up their nights, weekends, and personal lives to build your company. Don't be upset when they stop short of doing what you'd do to get a project out the door.

There's only two ways to get employees to up their commitment to your company and act like owners, and that's to share the equity or to share the profits. I've seen good employees become outstanding minor equity partners. Their level of commitment and effort rises sharply when the owner's business and dream becomes theirs too. Staff also find incentive and motivation to improve their performance when they know their efforts could result in bigger shared profits each quarter.

An equity purchase plan raises the stakes. If you're looking to inspire your own level of commitment in most employees, then by all means, up the ante by offering equity. If you don't take it to that level, then you can't expect your team to share your degree of motivation and commitment. And that's alright, too. Just understand where you stand, and where they stand.

THREE LEVELS OF COMMUNICATION

There are three key levels of communication every business leader needs to master in order to make their company succeed. None of the levels work entirely on its own, but in combination, the three levels—State of the Union, Day-to-Day Communication, and Coffee Talk—are a winning communication strategy.

Let's look at each level from the broadest to the most individually focused:

Level One: State of the Union: Just as the President of the United States needs to reach out to the entire nation in a State of the Union Address, a business owner needs to update stakeholders and staff about the company's vision, successes, and plans for the coming period. A president addresses the nation once a year, but a company leader needs to communicate more frequently, either on a monthly or quarterly basis. The entire constituency, from frontline staff to stakeholders, needs to know that a clear direction is charted, a plan is in place, and someone is in charge.

The company team needs direction, both for assurance and to keep everyone on board with the business strategy. It's essential to not have outliers undermining the strategy by taking matters into their own hands. A company's "State of the Union" keeps everyone "in the know" all at once, and refreshes everyone's commitment to the same vision and goals, both short term and long term.

Level Two: Day-to-Day Communication: Timely communication on a daily basis is what keeps a company's strategy on course. A good organization uses information systems that create a strong cadence of ongoing communication, including messaging, reports, meetings, and team huddles. Ongoing daily and weekly communication keep staff informed on a need-to-know basis so that immediate challenges can be addressed and goals met. Timely updates keep people primed for tasks that need to be performed in an orderly, structured fashion to bring actionable outcomes.

Leaders need to communicate effectively about problems as they arise, so that individuals and teams can organize around quick solutions. Facts on the ground need to be managed and updates provided as necessary for staff, clients, and vendors. Without regular, day-to-day communication, small challenges can aggregate and stall a business. Finding the effective cadence of when to have regular updates, quick face-to-face meetings, and timely data reviews is key. Ongoing communication is often the toughest to master, but without it, companies begin to slide down an increasingly steep slope of dysfunction leading to failure.

Level Three: Coffee Talk: When real connection and relationship among leadership and staff is lacking in a business, morale suffers internally, which also affects customer relationships. A company leader may have learned the skills of good day-to-day communication focusing on business challenges, data, and problem-solving, but deeper connections may be missing.

Communication about business metrics alone—How's that order coming? Did the shipment go on time yesterday? Did we get payment on the Smith account?—doesn't have the personal connection of "coffee talk." Meaningful interaction about what's really important in people's lives takes communication to the next level. When staff and customers know that you care about them and their families, they feel far more connected to the business, your vision, and the company's brand. Getting to know your people and letting them know that you care will go a long way toward making your business a success and more like family.

For example, I consulted with a business owner who spent all of her time on day-to-day Level Two communication. Nicole's business appeared to be succeeding, but over time it became clear that staff morale was low, and her company culture was floundering. I recommended that she implement Level Three communication focused on connecting with staff personally. Nicole wasn't naturally geared for personal interaction, so we had to literally organize her calendar with the names of staff she'd talk to each day written on the wall calendar for reference. We also had to train her in how to make small talk, to ask questions, and engage people. She started going down to the shop floor to spend five minutes a day talking to a staff member. She'd give her complete attention, focusing on the individual, not on work, and she listened. Within weeks it became apparent that morale had started to climb, and so did productivity. It was the personal key Nicole had been missing in her communication strategy.

In order for your business to thrive, work toward activating all three communication levels, and you'll see the difference.

REWARDS

———

I hate bonus programs. They are supposed to motivate staff performance, but instead they frequently do the opposite. A bonus should reward outstanding performance, but when everyone gets a holiday bonus regardless of their performance, the bonus becomes an expected entitlement that defeats its own purpose.

If for some reason there is no bonus at holiday time, or it's less than expected, motivation can get twisted on its head. The lack of a bonus draws a negative reaction from staff, which lowers morale and leaves people frustrated. Employees don't consider that profits are down and money is tight. They just want their bonus, in fact, they are depending on a bonus for holiday shopping.

Instead of yearly bonuses, I prefer individual rewards that are given for particular reasons, such as the completion of a project or great effort at a specific task. Bonuses that are a direct response to performance are far more effective as motivators. By definition, a bonus shouldn't be expected, the staff member shouldn't see it coming, it should come as a surprise.

One of my favorite examples of an individualized bonus comes from my years in the restaurant business. Our kitchen manager, Chris, loved to kick off the spring camping season with a long weekend in the mountains. On the day before he left for his trip we happened to see each other at the mall. I was there to make a bank deposit, and he was doing some last-minute shopping for camping supplies. We talked about his trip for a while, and we turned to go our separate ways, but then I stopped and said, "Chris, you've done such a fantastic job with your team and all of the catering jobs this month." I pulled out a $100 bill from my cash deposit and said, "Here, please take this cash, and get yourself some extra supplies, some beer, and really good steaks to cook up on the campfire this weekend." Chris was thrilled and rushed back to the store for some quality steaks.

Eighteen months later he told me, "Remember the time you gave me that $100 bill to go camping? That was incredible, man! I bought these amazing steaks that we cooked up and they were awesome!"

In that moment I realized that the personal bonus I'd

given Chris had been paying dividends for a year and a half. It wasn't the amount, but the element of surprise and the timing of the gesture that had an impact on Chris. That $100 was an emotional memory attached to an event.

I learned that bonuses need to be personalized in order to have impact. A gift card to a favorite store, dinner at a new restaurant, or a weekend away can carry more meaning than a traditional end-of-year bonus. A bonus check or salary increase may amount to thousands of dollars, but with some thought, creativity, and personalization you can have an even greater impact on a person's morale and motivation. A raise often amounts to just a few extra dollars in a paycheck, hardly as effective as an unexpected reward that stays in a person's memory.

Try giving rewards on random weekdays when staff are least expecting it. An average Wednesday morning is a great time to share recognition of a staff member. These types of rewards can be delivered in front of the team to reinforce the connection between rewards and specific performance on the job.

In my marketing agency, we had a monthly spin of the "Wheel of Rewards" with a prize on every section of the wheel, a takeoff on the *Wheel of Fortune* game show. Staff members were nominated by coworkers in our monthly staff meetings for actions and outcomes they created for customers, coworkers, or the company. Their reward was a spin of the Wheel of Rewards with prizes ranging from coffee cards to free airline tickets. The possibility of winning something big, and not knowing what the prize would be, added to the effectiveness of the reward experience. It was an event that recognized great work in a dramatic way, far more effective than a yearly holiday bonus.

Semi-regular rewards, surprise bonuses, and peer celebrations can prove much more successful for boosting morale, motivation, and incentive. It's not about the dollar amounts, but rather your commitment to recognizing superior effort and performance.

THE BUS TEST

Back when I was in the software business, we always spoke about the inherent risk of losing our lead developer and not being able to pick up the pieces to complete our software code. Ian was an outstanding developer and fiercely independent. He could singlehandedly code any solution, and do it fast. The problem was that rarely did anyone know the specifics of Ian's coding and how it worked. This dynamic created job security for him, but at the same time, it put our product and company at risk.

This quandary became known conversationally as the "bus test." If a company's lead developer were to get hit by a bus tomorrow, what would be the status of the software or the company? Who else on staff knows enough to continue the coding? For anyone in software development, redundancy of resources and shared knowledge of programming is essential.

The bus test holds true across all facets of a business. For example, the delivery of products and services can't be dependent on any one individual. Staff members are keepers of information that involves everything from vendors and customer preferences to shipping details, invoice specifics, and payment terms. People hold details in their heads that relate to every corner of your business.

Think of the barista at your local coffee shop where you stop every day on the way to work. They know the specifics of your order without having to ask: half pump of vanilla, extra hot, with room for cream. Imagine stopping in tomorrow and your barista is no longer there; instead, you've got to detail your order preferences and nervously hope the new person gets it right. Your convenient coffee stop now requires that you train a new barista.

This is why redundancy of roles, responsibilities, tasks, and anecdotal information is vital to business operations. The details that individual staff members hold need to be clearly documented and effectively shared with a second and third person, and double-checked. Desk by desk, week by week, it's important to capture, retain, and share the knowledge your team holds. Get people to document and train another staff member—their "bus test buddy"—in the details of their role and the information they hold.

Keep in mind that some people don't want those

details known by others. They perceive it as their own job security—and that's the very point! From the start, therefore, build redundancy and interdependence into your company culture. Develop a company Wiki of client information, past projects, and key learnings. Messaging from leadership needs to stress that the company values sharing of knowledge, because it's best for everyone, including the customer.

This policy better extend to the business owner as well. The number one reason business owners can't take substantial vacation time is because their job functions and company knowledge are held too close to the chest. If they leave for a week, all of their functions and tasks stop for that time period, because there is zero redundancy for their role. Sure, you don't want staff to see your bank account or know your passwords. However, critical information and tasks need to be shared and controlled with proper safeguards, trust, and redundancy in place, involving key people who can fill in for the boss when necessary.

Start looking at every person and staff position in your business today. Where does your company pass and where does it fail the bus test? Make sure that each person's role, responsibilities, tasks, knowledge, and anecdotal information has built-in redundancy. The continuity of your business depends on it.

ONBOARDING

———

Many companies have no orientation process for introducing new staff to business operations. All too often, onboarding consists of nothing more than showing a person to their cubicle and saying, "Here's your desk." After introductions at the Monday morning meeting, they are pretty much abandoned to fend for themselves. Fifteen days later everyone wonders why the "new guy" isn't doing very well.

For businesses to succeed and grow, proper onboarding of new hires is critical for two primary, interconnected reasons:

1. Onboarding immediately orients the new employee to their department, their responsibilities, and the operational systems the company uses. New hires need to be supported so they can hit the ground running and perform confidently at the peak of their

skillset. They need to be given the information, context, and shared company knowledge to succeed. When their performance is strong from the beginning, they receive the respect they need to excel and grow in their new position.

2. New hires need a clear understanding of the company's culture, policies, standards, and processes. These essentials can't be learned passively on the job, or from the wrong people, or independently while fumbling to make sense of things. A company should take the time to orient new employees to its vision, values, and way of getting things done so that everyone can succeed together. A peer "buddy" system is a great tool for this learning.

Some business owners think that once a new hire is clued in to the responsibilities and specific tasks of their role, they are fully informed. However, this is only the minimum a new staff member needs to contribute fully to the business. Employees need to be empowered to contribute to the culture through improvements to existing methods and systems, bringing innovations and best practices from their past work experience that could strengthen the team.

In my work in franchising, I learned that new people can be overwhelmed with information during their first month. New franchisees would come for ten days of training and leave excited, nervous, and seemingly ready to go start their own franchise business. What we discovered was that ten days of training was like drinking from a fire hose. People sort of remembered the overall concepts, but few could remember all the details of the many areas of business they were now supposed to be heading up. They suffered from information overload.

We realized that we needed to check back in with them at the three-month mark. By then, they had an idea of what they knew, and most importantly, what they couldn't remember. We would refresh, or completely redo, specific content areas for each person. The result was a dramatically higher success rate for the franchisees.

It's therefore crucial to sufficiently orient your staff members on day one, then regroup with them periodically to ensure that they have everything they need to know. The same holds for your long-term staff, as some develop bad habits, or as systems are updated. Everyone needs refreshers on policy, process, and why things are done in certain ways.

Companies neglect to upskill and reorient promoted people in their company too. For example, I worked with a high-profile museum that had seventeen departmental managers, most of whom had been with the organization for decades. Only one of those managers had any prior formal training in business or people management; the rest were just promoted and left to their own devices, squeaking by with limited management skills, and it showed. The performance of the museum was stagnant, culture and morale were terrible, and financially, the organization constantly fought to stay alive.

Ongoing training, group discussions, and upskilling needs to be a focus of your entire team. For your business to grow, you must constantly grow the people in it. Companies that consciously allocate time to people growth and skills improvement will leapfrog their competition.

JUST STOP WITH THE EMAILS ALREADY!

———

At the office with staff sitting only a few feet away from each other, I noticed they were still using instant messenger and email to communicate. I'd had about enough and heard myself yell, "Just stop with the emails and IM and just walk over and talk!" Their eyes got huge and fearful.

Was I being too radical?

In the increasingly digital world of communication, there is still an important place for in-person contact. In sales we recognize that most people still need some face-to-face time in order to feel comfortable enough to make a purchase. Yes, there is Amazon and many other online marketplaces, but the clear majority of consumer sales, especially major purchases, still occur through person-to-person transactions. Millennials may feel differently, but most buyers today still prefer the human touch for major purchases.

In the business world there is still a need for the emotional, human component. In fact, life coach and author Tony Robbins lists love and connection among his Six Human Emotional Needs. We all need human contact at work. We need the time and space to connect with coworkers through group meetings, collective lunches, brainstorming sessions, and teamwork events. We need to connect in person with clients and vendors to establish and maintain strong business ties. As every facilitator, trainer, and marketing guru knows, the basic human emotional need for connection drives a business's success.

It's becoming more and more common for people to hibernate in their cubicles for eight to ten hours a day using digital communication exclusively. This dynamic can be a soul-sucking existence that doesn't generate the highest performance or engagement. Work issues and problems are far easier to clarify and remedy through direct person-to-person contact. The rule of any organization needs to be: "We don't solve issues by email, we do it in person."

Get out of your chair, walk the ten paces to the other person, and say, "Let's talk about this." Unfortunately, the once common human experience of talking to someone about issues is becoming increasingly uncommon, and needs to change. Business owners can take the lead by promoting human connection in the workplace through their company culture. Yes, it is daunting to many people at first and certainly moves people beyond their comfort zone. It works, because as people discuss issues, they become more effective at finding solutions together.

When you build a team that talks, hashes things out, and solves problems in person, you are building a team of people that can do the same with customers, suppliers, and outside stakeholders. Encourage people to hone those skills as part of your culture. Demand it of them. Strong person-to-person communication skills will help them throughout their careers, even long after they leave your business. In the meantime, they'll make your business stronger and more highly effective and appealing to customers.

DRINK SCOTCH

———

My former business partner used to be someone who would let things build and fester emotionally until he'd blow up at staff or at me. It gave him some temporary relief to yell and maybe throw something, but it undermined relationships on our team. He didn't feel good about it, and neither did I. He was an absolutely terrific guy and I didn't want to see his relationships with staff damaged or our friendship strained due to his outbursts.

We agreed that we needed a system to bring things up before they became an explosive situation, so we developed what became a formal methodology. We called it a "Scotch Meeting" in which we'd manage our partnership, our friendship, and any pressing work issues before they had a chance to fester.

The format and method went like this:

- If an issue was bothering one of us, that person would say, "I need to have a Scotch Meeting." It served as a gentle notification that there was a problem that needed some discussion.
- The response was always yes, because as part of the process, neither of us could decline an invitation. We'd ask how soon the meeting was needed—today, this week, next week? The timing of the meeting was an indicator of the seriousness of the issue or the emotional intensity behind the request.
- We'd meet offsite away from the office, partly to get out of our surroundings, but also to be in a public place where we'd have to address things in a civilized manner—just like Jerry Maguire in the movie when he was fired in a public place so he wouldn't make a scene.
- We'd each order a Scotch. It could have been wine, beer, coffee, or soda, but we both liked Scotch, and it was a good icebreaker for us. The alcohol took the edge off, and we could discuss things more openly. We'd start the conversation after no more than one Scotch.
- The conversation would begin: "So you called this Scotch Meeting, what would you like to discuss?" The convener then had the floor until he was done expressing his concern or frustration. The important element here was the other person's commitment to listening without responding, because the invitee needed to really understand the problem at hand.

- We would then move to discussing solutions. Sometimes it was an easy fix, a simple suggestion that we could both agree on. Sometimes we talked at length trying to find a work-around. Sometimes we just ordered more Scotch and the problem seemed to dissolve until we couldn't remember it (because sometimes we just needed our business partner to hear us, and to personally reconnect).
- We didn't set ultimatums or demand that a problem needed to be solved in a particular way. It had to be a solution we defined together, one that worked for both of us, and one that we could unanimously support and put in place together.
- The primary rule was that we wouldn't end the Scotch Meeting without a solution. When we came up with one, we'd implement it right away to ensure that the issue wouldn't resurface or remain outstanding.

The Scotch Meeting protocol is one of the most effective tools I've ever used for managing the emotional component of business relationships. It has the capacity to move issues from a scary place of silence and growing frustration to getting things out in the open quickly and collaboratively to find solutions. It isn't a concept limited to just business partnerships.

In my consulting work, I've introduced the Scotch Meeting protocol to companies to use for their management teams, or sometimes across an entire organization. In these circumstances, we've found it better to introduce the concept as a Coffee Meeting. Of course, it needs to be understood that the meeting isn't a social get-together over a cup of Joe, but a friendly problem-solving session, whatever the beverage of choice. The intention and purpose of the meeting is very specific.

The Scotch Meeting protocol has generated more positive feedback and resolved more issues than my former business partner and I ever imagined. It is a fantastic tool for business owners and partners serious about their relationships and long-term success.

PART SIX

LEAD LIKE A LION, MANAGE LIKE A SQUIRREL

Leading a company and managing a company require two very different skillsets. Most people are naturally better at one or the other, and few possess both in equal proportion. For the entrepreneur, leading and managing a company is almost like having multiple personalities—lion and squirrel.

Leadership requires the ability to be a strong communicator, someone who sees the big picture and can inspire others around them, including staff, customers, and even the occasional banker. The leader is the lion of the business, exuding strength, confidence, and authority that inspires others to feel secure and willing to follow.

Management requires organization, attention to detail, collection of information, and interpretation of events. It involves a constant review of business feedback. The manager is the squirrel of the business; never wanting to lose or misplace a nut. They are always proactive and responsive, constantly assessing business operations and the daily situation.

Each role involves different timeframes. Leaders are looking to the future—tomorrow, next week, and next year. Managers focus on the present and past, but rarely on the future. They are evaluating what happened yesterday and overseeing what is happening today.

Some people think that good leadership trumps good

management, but both are absolutely essential and critical to your company. Don't try to cut corners in either role, unless you have a secret wish to sabotage your success. If you, as the owner, struggle with one of the roles, it's best to find someone to support you by filling that role. In this way, you can ensure in your business there are one or more people with the talents to lead like a lion and manage like a squirrel.

THREE LEVELS OF LEADERSHIP

When people think of leaders, they think of Winston Churchill, Martin Luther King Jr., or Mahatma Gandhi. They think of great speeches and people looking presidential or royal. But those are just the trappings of leadership, not the nitty-gritty. Beyond the speeches and ceremonies, leaders must have the vision to create change and inspire people and organizations.

Over my years of observing, consulting, and interviewing entrepreneurs and their teams, I've come to see that businesses require three levels of consistent leadership. These three levels apply to leaders in high-performing companies, as well as leaders beyond the realm of business.

The three levels of leadership relate directly to the three key levels of communication discussed in Secret

47. These three levels—State of the Union, Day-to-Day Leader, and Coffee Talk—need to work in combination for a leader to succeed.

Let's look at each level of leadership from the broadest to the most individually focused:

Level One: State of the Union: On a monthly or quarterly basis, it's crucial for you as a business leader to address your team and stakeholders to update them about your vision for the company, recent successes, and what you have planned for the coming period. It is very much like the President of the United States delivering a yearly State of the Union Address. It's an opportunity to demonstrate leadership as a show of strength, confidence, and determination. People need to see that someone is in charge, that your hand is firmly on the tiller, the wind is at your back, and the company ship is on course for growth, success, and increased market share.

Level Two: Day-to-Day Leader: On an ongoing, daily basis, leaders need to respond quickly, clearly, and confidently to problems and challenges. This critical skill is the hardest to master because small challenges can easily collect and aggregate into a monster, or tiger, that can overwhelm business operations. Effective daily leadership means keeping those challenges and problems separate, and solving them individually. It requires the ability to make multiple small, well-reasoned decisions communicated to the team for swift action. As a company grows and stabilizes, this day-to-day leadership becomes increasingly about empowering people to make decisions on their own using the tools and methods you advocate. This is the kind of daily leadership that inspires your team, and reassures staff, clients, and vendors that your company is running smoothly and efficiently.

Level Three: Coffee Talk: A company leader may have learned the skills of good day-to-day leadership that focuses on business challenges and problem-solving, but a deeper level of leadership may still be missing. A leader who addresses business metrics alone—How's that order coming? Did the shipment go on time yesterday? Did we get payment on the Smith account?—may be lacking a necessary level of personal connection to staff, vendors, and clients that comes with "coffee talk."

When real connection and relationship is lacking in a business, morale suffers. But when staff and customers know that you care about them and their families, they feel far more connected to your business, your vision, and the company's brand. Getting to know your people through more personal coffee talk, lets them know you care. This goes a long way toward making your business a success and more like family. People follow a leader that cares.

One entrepreneur I know is talented at delivering powerful State of the Union presentations that are just short of rock concerts with audience participation, shout-outs from the crowd, prizes, and awards. Those monthly presentations succeed in inspiring the team, but only for a short time. Inspiration quickly drops off and performance lags because there is no personal connection beyond the monthly rally. Most of the time, staff just feel like cogs in the wheel of the owner's business.

Contrast that situation with another company leader I know who schedules an entire day each quarter to check-in and talk personally with each member of his staff. At first his staff were concerned when he scheduled these conversations, but they were put at ease when they saw that they weren't about their work performance, but about connecting and relating. The effect of these coffee talks and jam sessions have proven positive for team engagement and performance. The owner finds that some of the best improvements and innovative ideas for his business have sprouted from these informal conversations.

It takes all three levels of leadership to be a strong entrepreneur and visionary. As a business owner, you need to touch the bases on all three—State of the Union, Day-to-Day Leader, and Coffee Talk—in order to reach home plate and score runs in the business game.

HR IS A LEADERSHIP ISSUE

———

When did leadership and human resources become two separate parts of a business? What business school decided that HR should be totally separate from management and leadership? When a company leader tells me they have an "HR problem," I tell them they have a leadership problem.

HR departments typically deal with hiring, compensation, benefits programs, employee conflicts, poor performance, and many other staff issues that directly impact a company's leadership and broad operations. Owners or managers who deflect these areas of concern to someone in HR, are basically passing the buck. What does it say about their leadership? Primarily this: "I don't care enough about that to deal with it."

In my advisory work, I'm always reminding company leaders that "business is people." HR issues therefore need to be front and center for leadership. Leaders need to be engaged and committed to employee management, because it sets the tone for company culture. When a leader is crystal clear about what is acceptable at their company and what isn't, people take it to heart. A leader who is wishy-washy, disinterested, and doesn't know how to handle conflicts, gets about as much respect as a substitute teacher. People respond to leaders who set clear rules and provide guidance, similar to a teacher or parent who commands loyalty and esteem. A leader who steps up to deal with the challenges of HR and people issues, will build a reputation as a hands-on, no-holds-barred leader who isn't afraid to get her hands dirty. It's the kind of leadership that inspires confidence companywide.

There is a functional role for HR in any company. I wouldn't advocate for any business owner administering their benefits program, running payroll, or managing the paperwork of their people. However, people issues and opportunities, career paths and tough conversations are the places where the owner, as leader, steps in and steps up.

MANAGEMENT VS. LEADERSHIP

———

People tend to think that leadership and management are one and the same. Unfortunately, they are mistaken, and it's a mistake that too many business leaders make. In discussing the three levels of leadership in Secret 53, I never mentioned management. That's because leadership and management are separate functions. As mentioned earlier, we lead like a lion and manage like a squirrel—but with different timeframes. Leadership is future-focused, while management is past- and present-focused.

Management is all about the day-to-day running of business operations. It oversees processes around customer interaction, orders, delivery of services, staff needs, and problem-solving, to name just a few. It looks at how the business has performed in the past (reporting) and what is happening in the now. Management focuses on maximizing operations, and the processes within operations, so that everything runs as smoothly as possible.

When a business experiences operational issues on a daily basis, it's a sign that management is weak and systems are poorly defined. When management is strong, operations run smoothly and staff and customers are happy. In fact, good management can almost look like lazy management, because when systems run smoothly it can seem that they are running themselves. Actually it's more like a flywheel in an engine collecting and storing energy while providing continuous power and momentum.

Leadership, on the other hand, looks toward the future. It looks for trends and factors that will, and may already be influencing and impacting the company. Leadership surveys the lay of the land and refines the business accordingly, communicating regularly with stakeholders, including staff, customers, and shareholders.

A business leader extrapolates information from data and reports to make necessary changes to the business plan and the company's direction. A manager uses those same reports to see how operations and processes need to change now in the day-to-day.

Most entrepreneurs either get lost in the big picture of forward-looking trends, or they get trapped in the minutiae of daily operations. The toughest task for an entrepreneur is to create the time and space to evaluate the business both as a leader and a manager.

One problem is that owners who hire business managers tend to think that their management role and responsibilities are taken care of. This is a big mistake. The hired manager rarely has the perspective, insight, commitment, and historical company knowledge of the owner. The hired manager therefore needs owner input, guidance, and mentoring to hone the ability to see beyond the surface of daily operations.

By necessity, strong leadership requires business owners to wear both hats: leader and manager. To varying degrees, depending on the skills and talents of the management team, the leader delegates responsibilities while maintaining continuous oversight of operations and planning.

GET A COACH AND ADVISORY BOARD

———

In my first company, we spent almost a year "playing business." We had the big office—way more space than we needed, including a boardroom for fourteen people when there were only four of us. We hired a receptionist based solely on her looks, we designed and redesigned our business cards, we gave ourselves big job titles. My partner and I were twenty-one years old and we thought these items were critical. We worked hard, but not efficiently or with clear objectives. We weren't generating sales or limiting our expenses, so after a year we needed to borrow more funds to keep operations going.

We brought together family members, friends, and our banker for a Saturday morning meeting to discuss our situation. We selected people with business experience who could quickly assess our issues and provide ideas and strategies on how to fix them. By doing so, we inadvertently created a board of advisors with perspective to see our business from the outside. We took their sage advice and accepted accountability by agreeing to meet again two weeks later to see what progress we were making. Immediately, we hunkered down to manage our expenses, focus daily on sales, and create a budget and a system for reporting and forecasting, while also reducing our staff. Soon enough, our business turned a corner; we started to sell more product and began to look like a real company with a chance for long-term success.

We found that an advisory board has many advantages:

- Connections to new customers, staff, and vendors
- Experience from which to learn (without spending your cash to learn it)
- Insight into issues and solutions you don't see
- Accountability to meet your goals
- Emotional and intellectual support

The last advantage—support—is really the most important. The support of an advisory board works on multiple levels; providing the confidence and empowerment of knowing a team of people has your back and cares enough to help steer your business right.

Your advisory board will meet with you monthly or

quarterly to provide strategic help and guidance. Yet a question remains: who will assist with the tactical details, accountability, and execution on a more frequent basis?

The answer: your business coach!

Now the title here might be coach, advisor, or guru. It might be business, entrepreneur, or leadership preceding it. It is someone that has strong business experience, strong insight, and great communication.

Every business owner needs a designated coach, the same way Tiger Woods has a golf coach. Tiger can crush a golf ball on his own, but he can't fine-tune his swing and technique without an expert watching from the outside. In the same way, a business coach or business advisor has perspective on your business that you don't. My own coach has commented more than once when bringing my attention to a crucial matter: "How can you not see this? You're a coach yourself and a business owner with five companies!"

I feel the same way when I'm coaching other entrepreneurs. I can see their business issues clear as day because I'm not emotionally involved. A business coach can be dispassionate when the business owner can't. It's not about intelligence, gumption, or skills, but about bringing objectivity and expertise to keep you on track and hold you to account.

A business coach can work with you weekly, or even daily, to provide the tools and insights to help you perform. In fact, a good coach or advisor is as critical to your business as a lawyer or an accountant. Your team of trusted advisors needs to include a great accountant, an attorney, *and* a coach, among others. Your coach needs to have operated businesses before, and should be equipped to provide you with practical and functional strategies, tactics, and resources. A good coach is not just providing some nice conversation, but affecting change, delivering ideas, and demanding performance.

Your business coach isn't a life coach or personal coach, but focused on business. (Of course, you can also have someone guiding you personally, but that's a different role.) Remember that along with a strong and experienced advisory board, a business coach is your ticket to success.

MANAGE YOUR PROFESSIONALS

———

It may seem counterintuitive, but your professional advisors—your lawyer, accountant, and bookkeeper, among others, all need to be managed. "What?" you may ask, "I spend $450 an hour on my lawyer, and now you're telling me that I need to spend extra time managing him too?" Yes, you do. This isn't to say that your lawyer or accountant aren't highly professional, it's just that they don't have the same broad vision of your business as you do. You need to keep them advised of important details, timelines, and pitfalls they might not see on their own.

Your accountant is great at helping you file your year-end taxes and prepare your financials. They may be able to offer some general advice on the business from those financial statements, but typically it is all rearview mirror work looking at the past. Many accountants don't proactively help you work through issues, manage into the future, or provide projections and budgeting. In order to get more than annual statements from your accountant, you need to be clear on what else you need, and ask them for it. You need to raise the bar on expectations and see that the accountant will meet the challenge.

Your lawyer is great at giving legal opinions, but typically knows little about running a company. An attorney who is a strategic thinker is a fantastic asset to you, but their scope in your company is limited. I've learned from experience to review legal paperwork for myself to ensure that everything makes sense from my own business perspective. As a business owner, after you do this often enough, you'll learn to understand all the "legalese." It's a necessary part of managing your lawyer, and well worth the effort to know that you're both on the same page. I also make it my business to be sure that documents are prepared on time and that any payments are ready when transactions are scheduled.

My favorite (or worst) example of this occurred as I prepared to close on the purchase of a pizza restaurant. On the day of the closing, I wanted to ensure there were no outstanding issues, so I called the buyer's lawyer and told him I'd stop by his office within a half hour to personally deliver the cashier's check for the purchase. I took the elevator up to his office and when the doors opened—

wham!—I walked smack into a locked steel grate. "Hello, anyone there?" No response. I rode the elevator back down and called him. He didn't return my call for an hour and a half, finally explaining that his office had been closed for the lunch hour.

"But I told you I was coming by right away!" After some back and forth I said I'd be back over immediately, and he said, "Well hurry, because I'm leaving early for a long weekend at the lake." I explained how the deal was set to close at 3 p.m., and he hedged. He said that we might not be able to get the signatures on time—that we'd have to push it off to the next week. "No," I told him, "we can't wait. I have staff and contractors ready to start immediately!" All we needed was a couple of signatures and confirmation of funds. It would take fifteen minutes by fax or email—signatures that we would have had hours earlier if he hadn't left for lunch when he knew I was coming.

Had I left the transaction up to him, everything would have been delayed. So, yes, lawyers and other professionals do need to be managed. You can't always count on them to get the job done in the way your business circumstances require.

A quick note on lawsuits: Avoid them! Even when you are right. Being right can be expensive, time-consuming, and draining. The modern legal system can drag your case around for months or years before you get to demonstrate how right you are. It can drain time, focus, and cash from your business. Instead, commit to finding the fastest and cheapest way out, and trust that karma will bring ultimate justice. Experience has shown me that what goes around comes around: everyone who has "wronged" me in business has had their own challenges later on.

Find professionals you can trust. Get referrals and testimonials, conduct interviews, ask the right questions, and request references. Hire your professionals the same way you hire staff, the process is similar. Some may think you're ridiculous for demanding so much, but their reaction tells you something about how they will approach your business. You deserve to work with the best, and only due diligence will get you there. It will also save you considerable time and effort when managing your professionals later.

PLAN FOR THE WORST, YOUR CONTROL HAS LIMITS

How much control do you have in your business? Probably a whole lot less than you think. With all the variables of staff, customers, vendors, investors, competitors, and consultants, along with the vagaries of the marketplace and events, there's a great deal beyond a business owner's control. You therefore need a Plan B for making decisions on the fly when outside factors throw a wrench into your daily operations or long-term plans.

I've seen all too many entrepreneurs unprepared and overly upset when outside variables disrupt their best-laid plans and expectations. What they fail to understand is that everyone has their own agenda, and the interests of clients, vendors, and many others won't always align perfectly with their own. Instead of feeling blindsided, business leaders need to be prepared to react adaptively, not emotionally.

Businesses have many moving parts and tools at their disposal to change processes, reorganize staff, launch new advertising, or adjust pricing, along with so many other options. The strategies and tactics of doing business don't happen in a vacuum. Anything from weather to government policy to competitor activity can alter the playing field. It's nothing personal, it's just business, which is always a complicated beast.

Sales is a classic example of how outside influences can ruin your master plan. Say you have a prospect, perhaps the biggest potential deal you've ever come across. You present your selling points, have meetings, and get to know the decision-makers. They love your product and want to buy. It's in the bag, everything is on track, you're dusting off your contract and preparing to pop the champagne when suddenly the deal goes silent. Three weeks later you get a call back telling you that your contact Doug suddenly left the company and senior management is freezing expenditures for the next quarter based on new financials. Some new guy on the team has sourced your product in China at half the price. For you it's a major comedown, but keep your perspective.

It's all in the game of doing business. Outside forces will create unforeseen issues that you need to be prepared for. Every critical piece of your business needs a Plan B. Who is your backup supplier? What's your backup hiring plan? Who are your other prospects? If you're depending on a single client or product to make things work, you're setting yourself up for a perfect fall. Don't go all-in on a gamble. You may win some hands at the poker table, but sooner or later you'll lose.

Instead, invest your faith, resources, and commitment in the long game, which includes backup options to cover any eventuality. Spend time regularly asking yourself about "doom" scenarios or variables that could fail. What if our shipments are stopped at the border? What if prices spike? What if our largest supplier ceases operations over the weekend? Playing out many scenarios and thinking about your backup plan or Plan B for every kind of challenge makes you more prepared.

Knowing your Plan B ahead of time is good business. It doesn't mean you should assume a negative posture; most of the challenges we plan for never occur. Ironically being well planned for adversity raises your outlook. Still it pays to evaluate, consider, and prepare beforehand so you stand a better chance of seeing what's coming and knowing what you'll do if it ever gets here.

PICK YOUR PARTNERS WELL...IF YOU NEED THEM

———

You and a friend are having a beer and come up with an incredible business idea. You talk it through and decide to quit your jobs and start a company. Your brother needs work and he's a good guy, so you bring him in too, sharing the company equity at 33 percent each. All seems fair, but what may not seem obvious is that this ownership structure is a recipe for disaster—yes, disaster!—regardless of how compatible the arrangement seems.

Getting into a business partnership is like getting married, except you'll probably spend more time with your work spouse. Unfortunately, people dive into business partnerships as if they are one-night stands, instead of a lifetime commitment (or more likely a five- to ten-year business life cycle commitment).

Choosing a business partner takes some serious dating before you tie the knot. You need to know a whole lot about whether your interests line up. How about a background check, an Interpol sweep, ten references from work and personal connections, a review of their social media pages? Maybe that's going too far—or not far enough! The point is to know what you're getting into. Even then, you still may not be able to work with the person due to different work styles, business philosophies, or visions for where the company should go.

I am telling you this from experience. I have agreed to business partnerships because we went to college together, our wives were friends, or we were good buddies who could both bartend. Often I've ended up in partnerships simply because someone asked me to join. This lack of sufficient scrutiny and forethought always led to issues later.

So, before you enter into a business partnership you may regret, here are some rules for a happy marriage:

1. Plan for your divorce as you enter the partnership; negotiating terms in your "prenup" will be much easier early on when you're relaxed, level-headed,

and cooperative. While you're still in the "love" phase, talk things out and have legal documents drawn up, in case you later decide to go your separate ways.

2. Try "living together" in a less permanent business structure before taking your vows. Consider working as a joint venture, alliance, or just a semi-casual working relationship for six months to test the waters. There are many partnership options outside of formal equity partnership in a corporation. In this way, you can explore how well you work together and evaluate the long-term potential.

3. One partner should have control of the company with at least 51 percent equity. When push comes to shove you'll probably want it to be you. Personally, I always want to have a majority stake in company partnership in order to carry the weight in decision-making. Owning a minority stake (49 percent or less) in a business means you are along for the ride, but the weight of your opinions is limited. If you need to put in more capital to get the majority stake, do so. It will be an awkward, but necessary negotiation that will save a lot of conflict in the future. Problems, such as gridlock, arise when partners have equal equity (see #4 below).

4. If you decide to go 50/50 or 33/33/33 or 25/25/25/25 then you need to have a decision-making escalation plan. When equity is evenly distributed, partners will eventually come to gridlock over some issue. How will a decision be made if there's no majority? Will

you bring in an outside party? Rock, paper, scissors? Make sure you have your plan for decision-making in writing (and please don't use rock, paper, scissors as a decision-making tool).

5. Don't give equity or partnership to just anyone. In a previous company, my business partner and I owned 95 percent. He felt strongly about locking in our three key participants and suppliers by gifting them 5 percent of the equity. It wound up strangling our business. Minority partners can gum up the works; they may want to attend meetings, or have a company expense account, or draw an equal salary. It's not worth the trouble.

6. Document the relationship. Make sure to have your lawyers and advisors review and coordinate your partnership agreement, share structure, and signing-authority arrangement. Too many entrepreneurs and partners fail to do this upfront. Five years later when the partnership is disintegrating, it's too late, no one will sign or commit to anything. Before operations start, make sure everyone signs on to a sound structure with rules to play by. (I know, you're probably looking for your lawyer's number right now, realizing you still haven't done this.)

7. Know your role. Just because you're a partner in the business doesn't mean your role is anything you want it to be, whenever something interests you. This happens all too often. Partners think that because they

own a share of the business they can get involved in every decision and area of the company. It doesn't work that way. Each partner's daily functional role in the business should be clearly defined. Who will be the sales manager and who will see to order fulfillment and shipping? Which positions will go to staff? Of course, owners need to know what is happening in all areas of the business, but for day-to-day operations, partners need to be focused on specific aspects that align with their skills.

Partners are people who bring unique skillsets critical to a business' vision, planning, and daily operations. Choose your partners carefully with an eye to filling voids in your own knowledge and experience. Business partnership is about long-term compatibility and commitment, just like a marriage.

ON VS. IN

In his book *The E-Myth*, entrepreneur and author, Michael Gerber, famously coined the phrase "work *on* your business, not *in* your business." He was referring to the common mistake entrepreneurs make of getting trapped in the day-to-day operations of their business, instead of concentrating on building and growing their company.

It's an easy concept to grasp intellectually: business owners tend to get caught up in micromanaging the daily details of operations, when they should be tending to long-range planning and strategizing. The immediacy of troubleshooting winds up taking so much of a business owner's time that there is little time left over for envisioning where the company is going. To build successful, forward-thinking companies, entrepreneurs need to step out of day-to-day micromanagement, delegate those tasks to their team, and free themselves up to fully embrace their leadership role. Easier said than done.

In my coaching work with entrepreneurs, I've developed several tools to help business leaders work *on* their business rather than *in* their business:

- **Start in Your "Third Place" on Mondays:** Your "third place" is somewhere that is not your office and also not your home. Start your Mondays at a local coffee shop where you can sit back with a fresh brew and take some time to review your goals for the week, including the specific actions you want to focus on to move your business forward. Take stock of what you can do this week for the business' growth and development. It may be one specific thing, or it may be five to ten items, depending on complexity.

- **Take a Day a Month:** Schedule an entire day out of the office each month to work on strategy and big-picture items. In this concentrated timeframe, work without distraction on your vision for the company, strategic initiatives, and priority of action. Many entrepreneurs I advise have a hard time believing they can schedule an entire day out of the office, but I remind them to think of it as an emergency. Before your business becomes an emergency, take a day each month to plan your company's forward momentum. Ensure your company's future by knowing where you're going and how you'll get there.

- **Blocks of Strategy Time:** A tip from my business coach Steve Leach is to block two to three hours on my calendar each week for "Strategy Time." Sometimes it's alone time, but other times I meet with other entrepreneurs, experts, and staff to brainstorm business growth strategies. Let your team know that this Strategy Time is necessary and crucial to company planning, as well as to the future of the business and everyone you employ.

· **Stay Away:** What many of these tools have in common is the need for an entrepreneur to carve out time away from the office. In order to work *on* your business, you need to take some distance from operations, staff, phone calls, email, and the many other continuous distractions of the workplace. Rent a boardroom at a hotel, go to a library, a garden, use a friend's office; just make it your business to get away to a quiet place where you can focus. At minimum, lock your office door and hang a sign that says, "Strategic Genius at Work."

Working on your business takes the kind of concentrated thought and planning that will take your company forward step by strategic step. You are looking to actuate improvements in systems, procedures, marketing, product development, and growth. You'll need to involve your team to execute your strategies, along with the specific actions and tactics to bring your ideas to fruition both short term and long term. For example, manufacturing improvements will require bringing your manufacturing supervisors into the discussion. The details of cash flow improvements can only be worked out in consultation with your controller or accountant.

Getting others involved provides you with the critical perspective needed to make your strategies more effective. Brainstorm on your own as much as possible, but you'll also need to bounce your ideas off others on your management and advisory teams. If you're like me, you'll probably need some conversation and feedback to help your ideas take shape. Collaborative thinking and sharing can open up new levels of inspiration and creativity to more completely flesh out your ideas and plans for change, growth, and expansion.

Our society embraces doing, often at the expense of thinking and planning. Moving twelve boxes of stock can feel more productive and valuable than brainstorming a method that will redefine your stock inventory system. Yet that new system will have broader dynamic impact, long term. For a business leader, strategizing is by far the most valuable activity to spend time doing. You'd never see the CEO of a major company bragging about their contribution on the production line or the number of customers they took orders from today. They know that their value is far removed from day-to-day operations.

Carve out time in your schedule now to take a fresh look

at your business. Work *on*, not *in*, your business every day, week, and month. You'll come to see that it's what leads to growth, improvement, and scalability.

ONE-PAGE PLAN

A good strategic business plan shouldn't be a paper-weight. Perhaps your banker has convinced you that your business plan should be a giant document in a big black binder. Years ago when I was forming my first software company, my banker took my business plan in his hands, hefted it up and down to get a sense of its mass, and told me, "Good plan!" He never even cracked it open to read it! He simply added it to our banking file and it never saw the light of day again. It may have served his banking purposes, but it didn't serve me.

Verne Harnish, founder of the Entrepreneurs' Organization and Gazelles Growth Institute, and author of *Mastering the Rockefeller Habits*, maintains that a good business plan should fit on a single sheet of paper. He calls it a One-Page Strategic Plan, and it's a great idea for several reasons:

1. For a plan to fit on one page, it needs to be highly focused and refined. Too many plans start on a bar napkin, but then proceed through review and revision until they grow weighted with too much detail and specificity. By then a plan's usefulness is limited. Heavily weighted plans need to be scaled back in order to be actionable.

2. For a plan to fit on one page, it needs to be clear and simple. Making a business complicated is easy, but making it simple and efficient is hard. So do the hard work to make your plan simple. In raising venture capital, VCs will tell you that your explanation and pitch for the business needs to be clear and simple.

3. In the age of social media and short attention spans, no one wants to read one hundred pages of drivel outlining your business. People will, however, be drawn to a business plan that can be summed up in a two-minute read of a single page of solid ideas. Your team of investors, advisors, and managers will be more likely to embrace such a plan.

4. It's important to review your plan frequently, which is far easier when it's short, sweet, and to the point. You don't want your plan to be a heavy tome sitting on a bookshelf. It should fit in your pocket and on your laptop without the need to scroll through pages. Take it with you on your smartphone and review it often to stay focused.

5. Your one-page plan should crisply and clearly define

and summarize your business strategies and tactics. As an example, instead of a plan just stating that you need more "marketing," concisely indicate your marketing strategy and tactics, a key means of measurement, and, if possible, who will oversee them. The longer, finer details can be saved for your marketing program brief.

Your one-page plan can be formal or informal. To get started on a one-page plan, simply take a sheet of paper and list ten actions, decisions, or conversations you need to accomplish in order to move your business forward. Over the next ten weeks, make it your business to accomplish each of those items, getting one done each week. Review the list daily, carry it with you, and make one item your focus at the start of each day. Do this and you'll start to see immediate improvements in your business. Get your team involved, as well. Let them know which item on the list is the goal for that week, and what they need to do to help get it done. Watch how they spring into action when they know that the step is critical to the business and its success.

Use your monthly strategic "on-the-business" day to review and make any necessary changes to your one-page plan to keep it current and focused on the next stage of success.

RULE OF 88

———

I met an entrepreneur who'd been working for several years on illuminated house numbers that could be easily seen from the street. "How many have you sold so far?" I asked him. He said he hadn't sold any yet, because he really wanted to make sure the design was the best it could be. Within a year I saw a similar product for sale at Home Depot manufactured by another company. While the aspiring entrepreneur was busy perfecting his design, a competing business had already taken its product to market.

Perfection is sometimes better known as "analysis paralysis." All too many potential entrepreneurs spend too much time developing the perfect product to launch at the perfect price, on the perfect day, into the perfect distribution channel. In the meantime, they miss the boat.

They never heard of the "Rule of 88," which states: the time and effort it takes to get something to a degree of

88 percent *competent* completion is the same quantity of time and effort it will take to bring it the last 12 percent to *perfected* completion.

The market moves too fast for perfect. If you can get a product to a state of 88 percent excellence, it's ready to launch as is. Don't delay by starting down a whole second cycle of development, doubling your time trying to make it "perfect." Most people don't care about perfect. Perfect is too expensive. Perfect will kill your business.

Launch your product or service, get it working and into the hands of customers to evaluate and provide feedback. Tell them it is a prototype, if it makes you feel better about it. In this way you'll get the ball rolling as a functioning, profitable business while you work on improvements for version 2.0.

If your kids earned grades of 88 percent on every school exam, it would make them honor roll students, and you'd be bursting with pride. The same holds for your business: 88 percent is in the ballpark of excellence.

If you, or anyone on your team, is constantly working for perfection, they need to get a poster, T-shirt, or tattoo of the number 88 as a reminder of the real goal. Remember, excellence moves business forward, perfection kills it dead.

MAKE THE CALL, RIGHT OR WRONG

The biggest killer of your business won't be wrong decisions, but no decision at all. The path to an organization's death is strewn with discussion, analysis, more discussion, and more analysis, deferring decisions to tomorrow. Like a shark, a company needs to be constantly moving in order to breathe and survive. It is considerably easier to make corrections while in motion than from a standstill. Inertia is a business killer.

From now on, your fear of making the wrong decision should be overshadowed by the real threat: not making a decision quickly enough. Dragging your feet on timely decisions is a barrier to success. In an age of information overload, there will always be more data to gather, so don't delay. As Andrew Carnegie said, "Most people will lose more to indecision than they will to a bad decision."

In order for a company to grow and improve it has to be constantly changing. Part of your weekly and monthly review should include a quick look at recent decisions and how they have influenced your business momentum. These timely, short reviews allow for rapid reassessment of your path and decision-making. If nothing stands out as having been drastically wrong, then keep going. Use the information you have at hand to make decisions as they become necessary. You can make adjustments later if you really need to. The combined action of your decision-making and the small changes that result will help your organization evolve day-to-day.

A business, depending on its size, requires thousands of decisions over its lifetime. Don't hamstring yourself by thinking that every decision is a major one. Decisions are a regular part of the business process with numerous microdecisions occurring hourly, daily, and weekly. Businesses are constantly adjusting and readjusting, adapting, and readapting to conditions on the ground.

Learn to trust your gut by practicing a fast analysis and decision-making process. Trust yourself as the director of the company to know what to do. Heck, make it fun like a game show "lightning round" of decisions with your team to practice and strengthen decision speed. Making quick decisions will lead to faster growth and a more nimble, empowered organization.

BEVERAGE MANAGEMENT

———

You call a management meeting and everyone seems more concerned about managing their beverages—topping up their coffee, getting water, heating some tea, grabbing a soda—than participating in the meeting. For them it is a Beverage Management Meeting first and foremost. In a company striving for growth and performance, this lack of focused attention is an issue of concern.

Something needs to change.

First, staff need to be challenged to bring materials, deliver reports, and provide updates. Meeting participation should come with the expectation that staff members will present to the group and answer questions.

Second, the responsibility for running the meeting needs to be shared and rotated. Sharing the honors in this way increases engagement, as each person gains experience as a moderator. Periodically assuming the lead brings each participant closer to the purpose, value, and function of the meeting. Also, no one wants to be in the spotlight unprepared, especially when there will be questions. The meeting needs some degree of preparation, presenters chosen, reports printed. This new dynamic opens opportunities for guidance and mentoring by you and other managers to ensure that meetings are productive and moderators are well versed.

I can promise you that once a team member has been tasked with running a meeting, they will always have a higher level of involvement and participation afterward. They develop a deeper understanding of what's involved, what's at stake, and what it's like to be in the hot seat of the meeting chair. You'll find that participation will skyrocket and future meetings will be far better attended, productive, and enjoyed.

There are many variations on the traditional meeting that can also spur interest and participation:

- Five-minute huddles where no one sits
- Updates to boards or graphs where everyone gathers around (again, no sitting)
- Key metrics boards that everyone can see 24/7
- Key updates sent via bullet-point emails

The faster you get away from people sitting for long periods of time in meetings (I recommend twenty minutes), the faster your team can get back to work and the business of growing the company.

FLY UNDER THE RADAR

___

On your way to building market share, don't wake the sleeping giant of your competition. All too many start-ups get hung up on flagrant, ego-driven self-promotion. Entrepreneurs get sidetracked by thinking they need to be busy building their business with every PR stunt, awards program, and online profile they can get. They chase the goal of broad recognition, stirring up trouble for themselves, instead of leading by outperforming and out-servicing their competition.

By all means, make your business terrific, but don't get caught up in over-promotion of yourself or the company's profile. Trying to take the market by storm can be a red flag to your largest competitor. An established company can fight off newcomers by slashing prices and giving away services for as long as it takes to eliminate you as a threat. Instead of overplaying your hand, it's far more strategic to gradually gain market share. Build your client base without your largest competitors even knowing you're there.

Targeted marketing to your client base is more effective than plastering your face on billboards. Ideally, you want to focus your efforts on an outstanding client service program that builds loyal customers who will tell other people about you. The idea is to gradually attract clients away from the largest market players, until one day they realize that they've been hearing your name a lot. By the time they start looking into you, you've already stolen away so many clients that they can't roll back the tide.

I know a business owner who got into the linens rental business for the hospitality industry. Nathan began to take clients away from a larger national competitor at a healthy pace. The competitor didn't really notice because they had hundreds of accounts. Nathan was approached for an article in the local paper about his success, but he declined. Instead, he focused on gaining clients and broadening his services. When he was nominated for an award and approached to run radio ads promoting his success, he declined again. He knew where his prospective clients were, and quietly kept gaining them one by one.

Finally, his national competitor woke up with a call from the head office to the rep: "Who the hell is this company stealing our accounts?" But it was too late. Nathan had a foothold in the market and enough reputation among his clients that he had momentum and competitive advantages. Now he could invite a little fanfare and bring some recognition to himself.

Until you are a stable, midsized player, you'd better tend to business: your product, your vision, your customers, and staff. If your performance generates media attention, that's fine, but don't go rushing to publicize yourself. Fly under the radar until you're big enough to compete and win in your market.

REPEAT UNTIL THEY MOCK YOU

Many business owners and managers muddy the waters by swamping their team with too many competing messages. Staff members catch on quickly that the message this week is fleeting, and the next week will bring a new message with a new theme. There are, of course, many ideas to share with your team, but key messaging needs to be consistent and focused in order to be effective.

When staff are bombarded with different messages weekly or monthly, they can't focus on which to make a priority. They move from one to the other until it becomes impossible to keep up, so they try to stay neutral by following none of them. Imagine working with a trainer at the gym, and each time you begin an exercise, the trainer starts telling you about the next exercise or insight. "Push-ups are the best exercise." "You need to focus on your legs." "Stretching is the most important thing each day." "Do more sit-ups." It can be confusing and cause you to lose concentration in both body and mind. All of those starts and stops going from one exercise to the next is entirely self-defeating and hardly a way to make gains at the gym. You need to focus on one exercise at a time.

It's the same with competing messages at work. Staff don't know which way to turn and nothing is gained.

The solution is in timely, focused messaging that catches staff attention and generates action. This works best with three to four key messages that zero in on your main objectives for the year. Annual messages to your team are ideal when they direct attention to core goals that are repeated periodically to inspire and make the messages stick.

During the year, keep your core messaging fresh. You can drive home your key objectives by pointing out examples of staff taking the lead and living the message. Offer awards and prizes that recognize outstanding staff who exemplify your objectives in action. You'll start to see your key messages gaining traction, influencing your team and every aspect of your business.

Clients often ask me, "How do I know when staff are hearing my message frequently enough?"

I always tell them, "When they begin to mock you."

If you're a parent, you'll recognize a parallel here to dealing with your children. You give them basic rules and eventually, as you repeat the rules often enough, they interrupt you to finish your words in a mocking Homer Simpson voice.

It's the same with leadership messaging. When your team knows your message by heart and can repeat it like some kind of mocking mantra, you've nailed it. They know it and can start living it daily within your company, which is just what you want.

—

PART SEVEN

COUNT YOUR CASH

I never really cared much for accounting—until I had real money on the line. In university, I took entry-level accounting three times. I failed with an F, then barely passed with D+ (not enough to advance to the next course), until I finally scored a B+. Ironically, I'd aced high school math and I'm good with numbers, but accounting just bored me to distraction. I couldn't muster the slightest interest in the subject—until I started a company.

Suddenly I was watching cash like a hawk. I was concerned about every penny that went out and every penny owing that hadn't come in yet. I became devoted to the math of in versus out. I'd catch myself thinking, "Is this a balance sheet item or a profit and loss item?" Who was I becoming?

Gradually, over years of mostly bad decisions, I learned about cash management and the importance of finances in business, and in life. Along the way, I received great financial advice from many brilliant business people. However, I didn't always heed or even quite understand their advice until I'd done something wrong and realized, "Oh, this is what they meant."

Cash is the number one stressor for entrepreneurs. It's the piece of the business that most consistently wakes them at 2 a.m. (I call it the Entrepreneurs' 2 a.m. Alarm Clock). Finances is the area that holds the most fear and worry, like a constant knock on the company door or the business owner's skull.

Most entrepreneurs will say they are "mostly" aware of their bank balance, and "sort of" know what they are invoicing this month. They have a "feel" or a "sense" of their finances, but they don't really know their accounts receivable balance, and the current ratio is still a completely foreign concept to them. They haven't yet learned that understanding and micromanaging their business' finances is crucial to their job. Subsequently, profit eludes them.

I'm here to tell you: Don't settle for having a vague understanding of your financial numbers. Get involved and educated on the cash of your business, because it's your oxygen. Without proper management and oversight, your business will die. It's time to set some rules for yourself about how you'll manage and master your company's cash.

Few people have any formal training on cash flow. When I ask entrepreneurs and business owners where they learned to manage their finances, the universal answer is "nowhere." As a group, business owners are fumbling their way through the cash management of their companies. They are often given bad advice from a banker or accountant, most of whom have never been entrepreneurs themselves.

Good cash management requires a certain level of self-ishness. As you grow a company, cash is always in short supply. It's therefore necessary to keep some funds on hand to pay staff and yourself.

Cash really is king. It's the lifeblood of a company, touching every organ and cell of the company body every single day. I've learned many lessons about cash the hard way. My hope in including the secrets that follow is that you'll have quicker success in financial mastery than I did.

CASH (MANAGEMENT) IS KING

———

Everyone in business pays some level of lip service to the importance of cash. We all understand the basics of providing a product or service and needing to get paid for it. The bottom line has always been cash out, cash in.

Most business owners get substantial direction about financial metrics to monitor and manage that aren't quite as critical as cash. For example, managing your balance sheet is an important, long-term equation. Most of your assets and liabilities don't shift values quickly, perhaps monthly at most. Your banker may be focusing on ratios and retained earnings on your balance sheet, but business owners only need to be looking at three things weekly: cash balance, current accounts receivables total, and current accounts payables total. These three items reveal your current financial state of affairs, and are exactly where you need to focus short term.

Of course, all financial and business health metrics are important, but when you manage cash first, everything else has a better chance of working. Prioritizing cash management gives you options when decisions need to be made.

In my work advising business owners, two issues in the management of cash stand out as the most impactful: distractions and bad beliefs.

Distractions take business owners away from paying close enough attention to the management of their cash flow. A primary distraction is business operations. Owners are told by advisors and so-called "experts" to measure operation metrics, such as inventory, customer service, and labor rates, while leaving cash flow management for last. They miss the point that cash must always come first. Without cash flowing, these other items become irrelevant.

The second issue with cash management involves beliefs and feelings about cash. Misguided beliefs can completely mess up a company's management of cash. The following chart demonstrates how beliefs and feelings influence a company's finances and cash outcomes.

BELIEF OR FEELING	CASH OUTCOME
You don't feel valuable	You over-discount and give bad payment terms
You feel insecure	You do the work and don't invoice for weeks and months
You value others over yourself	You pay everyone until your account is at zero all the time
You believe money is bad	You choose clients that likely aren't going to pay you
You believe keeping cash is difficult	You save nothing and constantly have unforeseen expenses

A company's cash position and cash flow are a direct reflection of the beliefs of the people running the business. This is why it's so important to be clear about how your feelings and beliefs are impacting cash.

Ask yourself these questions:

- Am I comfortable with what I charge for my service or product?
- Do I feel proud when I invoice clients?
- Do I feel like I should discount prices often?
- Do I hesitate to phone people or talk to them when they are late in paying?
- Do I feel guilty whenever I owe someone money?

How you feel when reading these questions can tell you where you need to change your beliefs. It matters because your beliefs are impacting your actions, influencing your team, and ultimately affecting your approach to cash.

How do you change your beliefs?

Gaining awareness and clarity about your beliefs is the first step. Once you recognize beliefs that aren't serving your business, you can spot and change the behaviors linked to those beliefs and see how they impact your management of money and the company. I'd recommend hiring a consultant in belief repatterning, such as my good friend Suze Casey. I've used her services for years to identify beliefs that didn't serve me, replacing them with new ones that did. You can visit her website at www.beliefrepatterning.com.

My last point about beliefs and cash flow relates to focus.

I consulted with the owner of a small printing company who was struggling significantly with her cash flow and business. We started with a tour of her operation before sitting down to talk. There was a giant stack of paper on the corner of her desk, and I asked, "What's all this?" She told me it was all the payables, invoices, and people she owed money.

When I asked where she kept her customer invoices, A/R materials, and cashbox, she said, "The invoices we've sent out are in a filing cabinet in the back. I don't have an A/R report, and the cashbox is under the counter in the back."

I didn't reply directly. Instead I asked, "What do you focus on each day?"

She told me she felt overwhelmed with how much money she owed people. She was preoccupied with payables, and there was never any money in the business.

"Do yourself a favor," I said. "First, take all the bills and invoices owing on your desk and stuff them into the filing cabinet in the back. If you're not paying them today, it's best to just get them out of your way. Second, get your stack of customer invoices and work orders, and put those right here on your desk. Then, get the cashbox out from under the counter, and place it right here on the corner of your desk."

"Do you really think that will make a difference?" she asked.

"I don't know," I said, "but let's see."

Six weeks later, her sales had increased by about 16 percent, and more importantly, she said she'd never felt so good about her business. She told me that she hadn't realized how many transactions her business did in a day, how many invoices got sent out, and how much cash was actually in the building most days.

I asked her about her payables. "I think about them way less," she said, "and last week we actually had cash to break out the pile and start to pay some of them." She beamed, her stress in the business had never been so low and her outlook so optimistic. With our little bit of physical reorganization, we were actually reorganizing her focus and her set of beliefs about business priorities.

Every day you need to focus on which items closely affect cash. Cash is king because it truly is the daily lifeblood of your business.

Ask yourself daily:

- What can I sell today and get paid for?
- Who owes money that I can collect today?
- What other sources of cash can I review today—A/R, inventory?
- What other steps can I take to get more money in?

When you start to carefully manage cash, it sets a standard that ensures your business gets paid in a timely way for the work you do. It brings cash to the forefront of opportunity every day, and creates a habit of strong management that transfers to other areas of your business.

If I ask a business owner how often they manage their cash, and they tell me, "Oh, I guess every week or so," I immediately know that cash is a likely problem. Their management of business fundamentals is too loose.

Don't make that mistake. Honor the cash that flows in and out of your business every day. Guard it and guide it daily and you'll increase your chances for long-term success exponentially.

BASIC MATH

—

Financial metrics in a business can be overwhelming and intimidating. There are so many aspects to review, compare, and track. When you become overwhelmed with financial ratios, reports, and analysis, just go back to the basics. Track your money in, your money out, and ensure there is a positive balance.

Most people can take a pen and write down their basic personal expenses, along with their monthly take-home income, but few do it. If they did, they'd know whether they have any money left over, or if they're overspending. This type of "napkin math" is also effective for your business, provided that you're accurate with your numbers.

I ran a strategic business planning seminar where a portion of Day Two was spent reviewing and planning using financial statements. As people worked on their planning task, one gentleman raised his hand. I came over, and he told me quietly and reluctantly, "I don't really understand financial statements or these accounting terms at all."

"What kind of business are you in?" I asked.

"Concrete."

"Do you know your annual sales?"

"About $10.5 million," he said.

"That's a hefty chunk of change. If you don't read financials, how do you manage the business?" I asked.

"I always just make sure the cash is going up in our accounts," he said. "I finish the month, look at what we sold, then look at our expenses to get the difference." He told me that he added it all up manually and kept a handwritten cheat sheet in his desk. He watched his bank balance every month to ensure it was growing. When cash went down, he got out and sold more product. When cash was going up, he knew he was doing okay, and he set a little aside each month.

He was a great business owner who found a basic system to manage the math of his business. He didn't need an MBA, and didn't need to understand complex finances to run the basic math of his company. While his calculations were basic, he was diligent about reviewing things weekly and monthly. In fact, his insecurity about his lack of financial knowledge made him more disciplined and focused. He reviewed his numbers and managed his cash consistently.

His technique was simple and worked for him, but there are many other financial controls and factors I'd suggest incorporating into your financial management strategy long term.

Step one is knowing and managing the basic math of your business. It's like dancing. You start with the basic box step before you learn turns, lifts, and swings. Your basic math should come in a weekly report, which is a summary snapshot of the whole business on a single sheet of paper or a single screenshot.

In the restaurant business, we would have a single weekly report that told us our bank balance, sales for the week by category, weekly purchases, inventory total, labor cost for the week, along with an empty field for notes. Seeing a quick summary with our basic math each week gave us the ability to spot any irregularities instantly. It gave us knowledge and control over the business numbers so we could adjust our management and decisions.

If sales were down we knew to focus on lower costs the

following week. If inventory was up, we knew to order less product in. We could manage the coming week based on a full summary from the week before. It was basic math, but essential for great management. I suggest you do the same.

FINDING HIDDEN CASH

What if I told you that every business had hidden treasure buried in its basement? I don't mean a chest of gold and jewels, but almost every business I've come across has tied-up cash, additional sales, and missed opportunities just lying around, available and squandered.

Most business owners think that hidden cash is only in high inventory levels or outstanding accounts receivable. These are the obvious places your accountant would identify, but they are only a starting point for when you need to free up some cash. Of course, you can sell off some inventory or collect money owed to you, but those options are often limited. Some of the larger sources of cash are not apparent on the balance sheet.

Hidden sources of cash actually exist in missed sales opportunities. You can control cash both through sales and in how you manage client transactions. These tools can provide considerable control and cash resources.

Here are a few hidden sources of treasure buried in sales:

- Longer-Term Contracts: Client agreements are often based on twelve-month contracts. I once had a salesman who joined our company and immediately started signing thirty-six and up to sixty-month contracts with clients. He actually had to handwrite in the terms because we didn't have those options on our preprinted contracts. His innovation extended and locked in our cash flow for years!
- Initial Payment on Signing: Most businesses sign contracts with clients, start doing the work, bill thirty days later, then wait an additional thirty to sixty days to get paid. Businesses sometimes have to chase payments down, establish an A/R system, and allocate time for doing it. Alternatively, what if your clients made their first payment as "skin in the game" from the moment they sign an agreement to work together? Step one on a sale is the initial payment. When every sale begins with cash on day one, you can use sales to immediately create cash flow in the business. No more delays of thirty to sixty days waiting to start receiving cash.
- Payment Upfront: Businesses often make payment plans available to clients in order to finance a purchase

or pay over time. Yet there are many opportunities to go in the opposite direction. You can offer clients a small discount in return for a portion of payment upfront for the first quarter, six months, or even an entire year. Some clients like the idea of prepaying for a discount on price. Offer it to clients as a "value-added" option and you'll be shocked when they say, "Okay, I'll pay for six months in advance."

- Secondary Sales: Many retailers and business-to-business companies have substantial accessory, secondary product, or add-on sales opportunities they aren't using. These are often higher-margin items that don't get the attention and sales they deserve. Mandate to your sales staff that when a customer buys your main product or service, the sale should also include a secondary product. We've all experienced such secondary sells of "purchase insurance" or extended warranties on everything from electronics to automobiles. These add-on sales opportunities have a massive margin pushed by everyone in the organization because it drives cash flow.

- Increase Deposits: Many companies are leaving deposit money on the table. Businesses typically contract for deposits of 10 or 20 percent to start a project. Why not increase that to 30 or 50 percent and give yourself a cash cushion on the project or product delivery (and eliminate the risk of negative cash flow). Many customers want to negotiate the deposit, so I start at 50 percent, knowing I'll settle for a "special deal" at 30 percent.

- Planned Purchases: Get your sales team and clients thinking beyond just a single transaction. Ask your clients about their plans to purchase from your company over the next six months, the next year, and beyond. Customers often know what they might need over time, so offer them the opportunity to plan those purchases in advance. You can often accelerate the speed of a purchase beyond the pace the client would use on their own. Then get a deposit on the whole amount!

These are just of few of the hidden sources of cash you don't already know you have!

COLLECTING A/R IS PSYCHOLOGICAL WARFARE

———

In my first software business, we had long periods of time between big value sales transactions. During that time I learned a lot about collecting accounts receivable (A/R) by learning how to dodge payment commitments. There were months when the only cash we had went to pay our critical bills. We had no cash to spare for anything that wasn't essential. Suppliers called all the time to collect on their invoices, but we had no money to pay them. Those calls taught me a lot about the major pitfalls of most collection efforts.

Many of the calls would go like this: "Hi, this is Darla from ABC Corp. We have an outstanding invoice, number

10934 from June 12 and I was wondering when we can expect payment?"

I would respond with total honesty, but with complete vagueness: "Darla, we have that invoice in our payables and we'll be processing it soon."

Darla (and most of the other collections people) would typically respond: "Okay, that's great, thank you."

But what had I really told her? What had I really committed to? Nothing. I never gave a date or time. I never explained what I meant by "processing it." I never clearly said I was paying it! Yet these calls and interactions went on for months. I could instantly buy myself another thirty days just by telling someone we were "looking into their invoice." I could stretch a payment for up to 120 days before many people ever said, "Are you paying this invoice or not?!" By then, I could comfortably say yes, because I had already managed a four-month delay of payment.

Knowing what it's like to be tight on cash and loose on excuses, here is how I collect on receivables. The key is to expect that the person needing to pay is going to be vague and noncommittal. Your job is to pin them down to a commitment. It goes something like this:

"Doug, hi, its Marty calling from ABC Corp. for invoice 10934. Have you sent payment for this invoice yet? You think so? Well, can you please check? I'll hold. Oh, so you haven't sent it out yet? Okay, when will you be making the payment? Next week? Okay, is that Monday or Friday next week? Okay, Friday. Will that be ready in the morning or the afternoon, because I'm going to send a courier to pick it up." (This is a great lesson: Don't leave it up to the postal system to collect your money. Control the delivery of your money by spending the $10 to $40 on a courier to go get it. Yes, it's an extra cost, but it's less than the cost of not having your money in hand). "Okay, so Friday afternoon? Terrific. Just to confirm, I'll be sending a courier over on Friday at 1:30 p.m. to collect the payment. Thanks for your help."

Now they have agreed. They've committed to a date and a time that we can hold them to. There's something about knowing a courier is coming that makes people more accountable. I've overheard them say, "Well, what are we going to do now? They're sending a courier!"

Your approach should always be friendly, yet persistent. A major pitfall for people trying to collect payment is to become personally upset and hostile. Once you sound angry, you'll be avoided. The key is to always be so friendly and upbeat that people feel bad if they don't return your call or talk to you. Call persistently, every second day or even daily, until you get the answers you want. Be cordial and warm, firm and persistent.

It's your money. You performed the service or provided the product in good faith. Don't let customers suggest that it's somehow your fault they haven't paid. This is a classic ploy involving role reversal. The company or person owing the money gets upset in order to avoid having to commit to anything. In these cases I ask directly, "Is there a reason you're acting upset with me, about the bill that you're avoiding paying?" When you call them out, it's hard for them to maintain the angry charade.

Hold them to their end of the bargain, which is on-time payment. If a customer is a problem regularly, invite them to find another supplier with less self-respect and cash sense.

MY FIRST ANSWER TO EVERYTHING: RAISE YOUR PRICES

———

Raise your prices. This is practically the first answer I give as an advisor to any business client or to anyone asking for good ideas in business. It's a strategic decision in every business I operate. If you want to play in the marketplace, play at the top end. Raise your prices.

Every time I recommend this tactic, the immediate push-back response is, "Oh, we can't do that, our customers won't like it." Absolutely wrong! When it comes to price, businesses tend to misread their customers. In fact, the vast majority of the time, customers don't even notice a price increase.

For example, say you're a customer who buys a widget

every month for $49.95, then one day its $52.49. Do you really notice the price difference? No, because mentally you still round it off to $50. It's effectively the same price to you. Does it stop you from buying? No, because you aren't that price sensitive about something you buy all the time.

But let's say that a customer asks why you raised the price. In that case, you and your team should have a reasonable explanation at hand. In the audio production business, we simply present the facts: "Yes, prices have gone up on a few items because we've had a pretty serious increase in our rent, taxes, and utility costs. We have absorbed some of the increases and had to pass some of it on to our prices." People understand that businesses have costs that tend to go up. Of course, there's the occasional wing nut who believes everything should stay at 1982 prices, but those aren't the customers you want to keep.

Prices shouldn't go up radically. Try a 3 to 5 percent increase, then evaluate what happens. Usually, what happens is absolutely nothing. Prices go up and business continues as usual. After a few months, once you see there's been no significant backlash, raise the price again by another 3 to 5 percent. Keep raising incrementally until you notice a change, receive comments of concern, or until you see you're winning less business in bids, quotes, and estimates.

An import factor is to keep the price high enough that it challenges you to offer more. Many business owners shy away from price increases because they don't feel confident enough that what they're offering really deserves a price increase. They believe they are offering average services or products that should be priced accordingly. Instead, raise your prices and use that as internal pressure to deliver higher-quality goods and services. Innovate so you can offer more to your customers and earn a higher price in return.

The power of raising your prices is that the additional monies go directly to your bottom line. A higher price is simply margin added on to provide additional cash flow to your business. Profits are often elusive in business because services and products are underpriced. Most companies can raise prices several times before clients and prospects even begin to notice and change their buying decisions.

Unless you start to lose deals consistently, I suggest leaving the higher price. I would lower it only if there is considerable pushback. The funny thing is that there is never considerable pushback. The increases are so incremental that people don't notice. If there is a little lost business, it is often less than the new margins. More profit on fewer deals is still good.

As an entrepreneur, if you want to increase profit, raise

your prices. If you want your statements to look better for the bank, raise your prices. If you need to stop using your line of credit for cash flow, raise your prices. Many different cash-related issues have one solution: raise your prices!

DON'T LEAVE THE ACCOUNT AT ZERO

———

Every business has accounts payable (A/P). It's a natural state to be owing suppliers a little bit of money. It's also normal to have people who owe you money (see Secret 70 for accounts receivable).

These are pretty basic facts of doing business, so why bring it up? Because most business owners aren't comfortable with the arrangement. They don't quite understand that having a little owing to you, and a little owing out, is typical for companies.

Many business owners are poor at collecting on money owed. They're worried it could damage a client relationship or prevent a future purchase. They tell me, "I don't want to have to ask them to pay." Yet the same owners are quick to pay out every dollar they have to vendors and suppliers, typically leaving themselves with a bank balance of zero.

If you receive a payment of $25,000 today, do you immediately turn around and pay it out to your own suppliers? If so, you're not prioritizing the people most important to your business. You, your staff, and your business operations should come before your suppliers. This means that you can't ever zero out your account. When $25,000 comes in, send out $17,500 in payments and leave $7,500 in the bank.

Business owners have told me, "I can't sleep knowing we owe money to our suppliers." They don't quite get it that owing money in business is standard. So get comfortable with it. Owing no one *and* having a fat bank account just isn't practical in an operating company. Business owners need to get used to that.

There are two main reasons not to pay out every dime that comes in.

First, you need to ensure that you have some cash available at all times for emergencies. Something breaks today and you need to repair it now. You should have cash in your business account to fix it. Too many entrepreneurs wind up paying for emergencies by going into their personal accounts and lending money to their businesses. It isn't a viable system because too often the owner never sees their money back.

The second reason is that as an entrepreneur, you need to become comfortable with having some liability and payables. As described earlier, it's a normal position to be owed a little money and to owe other people a little money. You need to get used to recognizing that your cash flow must serve the business and you first. Any supplier who expects payment *now* is unrealistic, and likely has their own cash management issues. Their issue is not your issue, unless you take it on. (Note that "a little money" owed on both sides of the ledger is alright, but massive imbalances between your A/R and A/P are definitely not alright and point to bigger business issues.)

Get used to putting yourself first. The concept of keeping your business account balance well above zero is an extension of "pay yourself first." Often when starting a business there is little to no cash, and it's a struggle. Many entrepreneurs, however, get used to running on a zero bank balance in perpetuity. You need to break yourself of that habit. It's crucial to have cash on hand in your account. For example, I have a business client who likes to keep at least nine months of operating cash in her business account at all times—that's about $220,000 in the bank—otherwise, she can't sleep. To me that's an extreme requirement for a good night's sleep, but it makes good business sense.

You need to start looking at your cash position the way your accountant does. Here's the equation: Accounts Receivable + Cash in the Bank – Accounts Payable = a Positive Number

If this equation is always a positive number, then you are running your business effectively.

In other words: evaluate your overall cash position and leave money in your account every day.

SECRET 73

OVER-FINANCE

———

A few weeks ago, I met with a venture capitalist who told me, "If one more tech start-up asks me for $1 million just so they can break even, I'm going to lose it! Why does everyone need only a million, and why do they just want to break even?"

My immediate thought was they want to be responsible by not asking for more than they need, and by minimizing what they borrow. They figure that breaking even is enough to pay what they owe, make payroll, and become self-sustaining.

"I'd prefer to see a company ask for $10 million," the VC said, "and show me how they're going to dominate the industry, get out in front of everyone else. I'd rather go in with more money and know it will really make them competitive, instead of playing small."

He had a valid point. It's true that in raising money, playing small doesn't serve the company or its investors. While $1 million is a cultural threshold (becoming a "millionaire" is still the measure of success) and it seems like a lot of money, these days $1 million isn't much capital resource in business.

Case in point: In 2007, when I was in the restaurant business, the market was bullish. The bank had just loaned us $700,000, and we'd raised another $250,000 from investors. We also had more people who wanted to invest. But we were already cashed up and oversubscribed, so I couldn't see any reason to take on more than our budgets indicated we needed. Within a year, however, the markets crashed globally. The bank wanted their money back, and I was suddenly in a hurricane of financial grief.

I started calling all those investors who had expressed interest a year earlier. They were people who had literally pulled out their checkbooks without even asking to see the terms I was offering. But none of them were interested now. My safe investment suddenly appeared risky. They were spooked by the market conditions and holding their money closely. Meanwhile, I was in a serious cash shortage to operate and cover start-up costs.

Could I have foreseen the global recession coming? Of

course not. Could I have budgeted a bigger cushion into our plans? Absolutely.

From that point on I changed my strategy. On every project since that time, I prefer to over-finance. I raise more money than I need, I ask the bank for more, I get more investors on board, and I budget for levels of catastrophe. I also want to be positioned to give any unused money back, so I set terms that allow me to do that.

In other words, I plan for "playing big." When a bank or investors offer to give me cash, I take it. Being cashed up gives me strength of position, choice, and options I can use in the future. I assume there will be opportunities I can't foresee that will require more capital. I also know that there will be unforeseen costs and other factors. Budgets will double past initial estimates and timelines will be missed.

If you decide to use the same strategy, here's a word of warning: know your numbers, your carrying costs, and interest rates. This is crucial, because over-financing has to be done responsibly. You need to be able to ensure that you can make payments on the money you borrow.

Raising money and knowing finance options can be complex. Hiring someone to advise you, represent you, or to liaison with banks can be a strategic move. Just make sure they agree that your plan to over-finance is both strategic and effective.

PRIORITIZING PAYMENTS

———

A pile of bills and invoices to pay doesn't feel good. It's stressful. It can even be depressing watching cash leave your account as everyone else's account gets settled. It can also be downright hard to manage. That's why I've developed a system for paying out bills and accounts payable. It works when cash is tight or when cash is insufficient to cover everything in your stack of invoices to be paid.

I start with a focus on relationships. Who are the vendors that I have strong personal relationships with? Which vendors are key to my business?

I once had a client who was paying everyone except their major vendor (because everyone else's bills were smaller). But not paying a major vendor is a poor strategy. It can put your whole business at risk. Therefore, it makes far more sense to pay your recurring suppliers first; those are the vendors with whom you and your business have strong relationships.

Ask yourself, how was the delivery of their services? I once had an IT company come in to do some maintenance. They accidentally broke a printer they weren't working on and took more than six months to fix it. Yet they wanted immediate payment for their service. Instead, I matched the payment to their response on the printer. Poor service doesn't get top priority for payment. I also recognized that the market had hundreds of IT companies I could use, so it wasn't a critical relationship.

Like a keen shopper, I ask for discounts. Not often, but I do ask for discounts when things aren't delivered right, or when I feel the final amount doesn't match the value that was provided. I initiate a straightforward conversation in which I clearly state my specific issues, and then ask for a reduction. I would say two out of three times, I get some satisfaction and a reduced cost by simply asking.

I often pay invoices in installments. If an invoice is a large amount, or if it's a delivery of services that is taking months, I break the invoice down into payments and send two or three installments over time to complete the payment. Most suppliers are good with this. Everyone loves full payment, but most businesses care more about cash flow, so timely installments (weekly or biweekly) usually works out just fine. When it comes to strategic payments, it's important to communicate directly with your suppliers to make sure they're on board with, or at least aware of, the arrangement. As a rule, I've found that suppliers have always been accommodating about this.

In really difficult times, I've had to be more dramatic with partial payments. In a turnaround situation once, we had months where our payables were in the hundreds of thousands of dollars, but we only had about $40,000 to 60,000 available each month to pay our bills. So we did calculations to figure out the percentage of the payables we could manage. We determined that each vendor could get a partial payment of 20 percent of their bill each month. By doing this we treated everyone equally to ensure they saw our determination to pay. We communicated this strategy to them and ensured they knew everyone was treated equally. It wasn't ideal, but people appreciated the level field of payment and the transparency.

Utility companies, cell phone companies, and large corporations are at the bottom of my list. Many bill into the future, so customers are basically paying in advance. My small monthly payment has very little impact on their cash flow and business survival. For example, I recently received a bill for cable services at a rental property that was fifty-nine days into the future. I had started the service one day after the billing cycle cut off, and within days received a bill for two months. Knowing that they bill like this, long before services are provided, I am always comfortable paying the minimum and ensuring there is a month still owing on the bill.

I encourage clients to do their payables only once a month. In this way they can really see their monthly cash reserve and determine more accurately what they can pay in total. Paying continuously never gives an entrepreneur true visibility on what they can afford or what cash flow will allow. Vendors need to know that getting paid immediately for every invoice is not an effective or realistic way of doing business.

Keeping your cash is just as important as making it. That's why using these strategies will ensure that you maintain a reasonable bank balance *and* some balance on your payables list. Vendors are worried about their businesses and you have to take care of yours. If the voice in your head is pressuring you to use most, or all, of your available cash to pay bills, remember your priorities in this order: you, your team, your customers, then your vendors. Vendors and suppliers are critical, but they can't jump the queue of who you look after first.

SCARCITY MAKES YOU BETTER

———

In contrast to Secret 73: Over-Finance, once a start-up is up and running, obtaining more cash for operations to run is usually not the answer. High-performing, growing companies never seem to have enough cash, and they feel that scarcity. Do we buy this or buy that instead? Do we pay for this or for that today? How do we grow if we can't afford the equipment? How do we improve the product when everything requires more spending?

Decisions need to be made, and options need to be weighed almost daily in order to keep things moving ahead. But too many companies believe they need more cash to spend their way out of problems.

They're wrong. Instead of cash to throw at its problems, what the typical small to medium business needs is creativity. When you're in a position of cash scarcity, it forces you to find creative and innovative ways to do business. This is especially true when obtaining more credit or more cash isn't an option. Companies find solutions out of necessity. It's under these circumstances that the best innovation and differentiation occurs. Scarcity can transform a business into a market leader.

Airbnb needed client feedback and input to determine how they could improve their business model and user experience. They could have spent more money and hired a firm to do telephone or online surveys. They could have asked their investors to give them more cash for hiring a customer liaison. Instead, they spent no substantial money and came up with a personalized solution. They knocked on the doors of their Airbnb hosts in New York and talked with them at length, even staying with people overnight at times. They offered the incentive of professional photoshoots (which they initially did themselves). They literally showed up and asked their customers what could be improved. They listened and heard their clients' ideas. Their solution was absolutely brilliant and cost-effective in the extreme!

Even if you do have access to a lot of cash and capital, it can still be advantageous to establish a system that keeps that money a little out of reach. Set up an account, such as a money market fund, that keeps cash beyond the reach of your daily checking account. Make it more difficult to access that money. Forty-eight hours is a good threshold for access. You can even put it in a short-term investment that would only give you monthly access. This will force you and your team to stretch your comfort zone and find creative solutions.

A distributor client of ours had been delivering their product in the same standard-size boxes everyone in the industry used. It was basically the shape and size of a shoebox. As the business grew, they were faced with the problem that their delivery vans could only hold so many boxes. They figured they needed to buy another van, but that option was beyond their capital reserves. So, they got creative.

One day while loading boxes for delivery, a driver casually said, "Imagine if these boxes were squares, how many more we could fit in the van." The owner instantly realized that boxes of a different dimension could allow for a bigger load. He sourced out a new box supplier that could provide a customized size at about the same price that would increase van space by about 35 percent. That meant three vans could carry more product than four had carried previously.

Then they looked at the vans they used, which were the same North American delivery vans their competitors used. They investigated van options globally and found a European model that could hold 28 percent more in the storage area. They decided to trade in the old standard vans and lease the more spacious model. By using creativity and innovative visioning, they solved their delivery issues with two quick solutions that didn't require spending more money.

But their story gets even better. Now, with their unique box size and funny-looking European vans, they suddenly had a look that differentiated their company from others in the city. They added some creative branding on their vans and boxes that caught even more attention and increased inquiries. More companies wanted to carry their product because people perceived them as new and innovative.

Use scarcity, or reservation of cash, as a tool to tap into your creative solutions capabilities. Challenge your team to find other ways to solve things before asking to buy a solution. Your business will prosper and stand out when you stretch these business muscles.

SPENDING RULES

—

I love spending money. I love buying new things, getting them home, and unwrapping them. I love the brand-new smell of a product no one has ever touched before. I confess that in business too, I've often been too quick to spend money on gadgets we didn't absolutely need. There are a lot of emotional justifications to buy most anything for your organization.

It took some time, but I've learned my lesson. So here are some foolproof tactics for managing and spending your cash, and curbing those emotional whims to buy, buy, buy.

- Spend Only What's in the Bank Today, Not What's Coming Tomorrow: How many times have you gotten a check for $10,000 coming in the mail, and by the time it arrives, you've already spent $7,800 of it. You start doing the math as though the money is already in the bank. You're saying to yourself, "Oh that check from ABC Corp. will cover this purchase." Except, the check in the mail doesn't arrive on time, and when it does come, the payment isn't what you expected. Meanwhile you've overspent your bank balance. Remember: Cash and payments don't exist until they are *in* your bank account unencumbered. I've seen banks hold payments for up to two weeks for random reasons. I've seen payments show up for half the expected amount. And, of course, I've stood longingly at the mailbox waiting for a payment that was supposed to arrive last Tuesday.

- Learn to Love Used Things: I never liked used things for all the reasons I love new things—until I learned better. I discovered that used things are frequently ideal solutions for my business. Used office furniture looks new. Used photocopiers work as well as new. Refurbished computers run the same programs. Your ego loves new and shiny, but your wallet loves previously owned. Used goods are a fraction of the price, solve your issues, and no one knows the difference. Every dollar saved on used solutions is a dollar you can put toward your bottom line.

- Shop Around: Get quotes, press for a better deal, and see what the market can offer. It's amazing how much you can save with a serious look at your options. The key to shopping around for the best price is efficiency. You need a solution quickly, and you don't have time for an exhaustive, painstaking, time-consuming hunt for the absolute cheapest option. Balance the cost of what you'll save on a cheaper solution with how much time you spend looking for it. It's like the $35-an-hour bookkeeper spending two hours to reconcile a $12 receipt. It just isn't worth it.

- Delay Everything: Next time a staff person comes in and says, "We desperately need a widget to do this," tell them "Sure, maybe next month," then wait and see if it's still essential after thirty days. Many of the purchases we rush into aren't necessary and don't save money or staff time. That's why I've implemented a policy of "Delay Everything One Month." After thirty days, is the new solution still essential or has it quietly gone away and died out, while operations have continued along happily? If it still seems valuable after one, or even two months, then you'll know it's time to lay down some cash.

- Who Can Buy It for You? There are many clever and strategic ways to get other people to pay for things. For instance, co-op marketing. This is when a supplier helps cover the cost of advertising and marketing because it helps their sales too. The same is true of equipment purchases that can be financed with your supplier or key vendors. They want to see you succeed because they want your business, and they often have deeper resources than you do. An example of this is 1-800-Got-Junk. When the company was starting up, its founder, Brian Scudamore, didn't have substantial budgets for marketing and advertising. They went to Mercedes-Benz and asked if the auto company would cover some of their promotion costs in exchange for featuring Mercedes trucks in their advertising. Mercedes agreed to cover the cost of the ads, and their trucks and logo appeared front and center. That's how Mercedes became the key supplier for 1-800-Got-Junk's global fleet of trucks.

In order to master your spending, look beyond the norm of what's usually done. You'll find cheaper and often better and more effective solutions. Make it part of your culture and your business profits will flourish far faster than you imagined.

BUILD YOUR PROFIT BUFFER

———

Most companies run on a financial strategy of "hope for profits." They get to the end of the year and send their financials to the accountant, then nervously wait to be told, "Yes, you did, in fact, make a profit." It's not a particularly effective strategy for ensuring that there's money left over at the end of the year, some actual payoff for all your hard, entrepreneurial work. Hoping for profits is a non-strategy that fails most small businesses year in and year out.

Yet there's a solution. I call it "Building a Profit Buffer into Your Business."

A break-even calculation for your business is how much revenue or turnover you need each month to cover your base expenses. Entrepreneurs can generally cover all their expenses through the year, but they rarely have anything left over. That's why I suggest adding an additional "expense line for Profit" to your revenue calculation.

Yes, you read me right: Add an expense line called Profit. You are going to pay your profit out like an expense every month to ensure it exists and gets accounted for. If you've managed to pay your bills until now, try adding a buffer for profit to your calculation and see what happens.

You will be withdrawing profit from your business' main bank account just like any other automatic bill payment. It will then go into a second account that will not be immediately accessible. Set it up at a different institution; make getting at the money more challenging to ensure it doesn't get consumed by business operations. Some companies are disciplined enough to simply carve off the "profit expense" to a second savings account. I'm not that disciplined. I need to keep it further out of reach. I once set up an account where my mom had to be a second signature for me to withdraw the money! Decide how far away it needs to be from your daily grasp to not get touched by operational cash flow.

A second, longer-term strategy for Building a Profit Buffer is what I call the "Gone to Shit" or GTS fund. This has been a business saving tool for me and my clients. Similar to adding an expense line for Profit and withdrawing it to a separate account, your GTS fund is another account you will not touch. You will regularly debit money out of your main bank account into an "in case of emergency, break glass" account. In this way you are self-funding your way out of an eventual emergency situation.

For clients who set up a GTS fund, it becomes a point of pride not to touch it. You'll now have an account that can get you out of emergency situations by simply writing a check or buying a solution. Most businesses have such high regard for their GTS funds that they hesitate to use them even when times are hard. They try to find another way. They've invested in that fund and want to maintain the security of it. As a backup plan, the GTS fund is empowering to entrepreneurs because it's always there.

A mentor of mine, Greg, ran a personal GTS fund (not part of a business), sweeping his personal checking account each month for 10 percent of what he brought in. Eventually his GTS fund had $600,000 in it. By then his goal was to never touch it and to be able to invest it for his children. Now, that's empowered!

Your business' GTS fund and Profit expense line can be withdrawn in weekly or biweekly transactions. It's best to make frequent and relatively small withdrawals, so you don't really miss the money. A weekly sweep of $400 is better than a monthly sweep of $1,600 (or $40 a week instead of $160 if you need to start that small). The goal is to overcome the common lament that "we don't ever have extra cash."

I worked with a client who had a cash flow of $250,000 through her business bank account every month. Yet, when asked, she said that her business didn't have the ability to put aside even one dollar because all of the company's cash was being spent on bills. Even so, she decided to give it a try, and we began sweeping the account weekly for $250, then increased it to $300. Soon the business had thousands in the second bank account and started to earn a profit. Meanwhile, they continued to spend everything that remained in their operating account. She learned that through a GTS fund and Profit expense system, she could ensure that some profit was protected each month, which totally changed her mindset.

Seeing and knowing that you are growing these two accounts can be a huge boost to your entrepreneurial confidence. We all, to some extent, measure our effectiveness based on our regular bank balance. Give these strategies a try and feel the difference that comes with being a solid operator and a good money manager.

PART EIGHT

GROWTH AND PERFORMANCE

Most entrepreneurs are trying to grow their companies. Few owners are just sitting back and avoiding opportunities that come their way. Yet a very large portion of owners who speak of growth are really only hoping for growth without any proposed plan or methodology for achieving it.

Growing your business takes a particular kind of commitment and mindset. A committed growth entrepreneur is future thinking, innovation focused, fired up for challenges, and highly enthusiastic about their company. When you talk with a business owner of this kind, you come away with a real sense of their commitment to growth. Entrepreneurs of this ilk can't look at any area of their shop or office without thinking about improvement and how to change things. They can't look at their team without considering performance, who is essential, and who will fit into the company's future. They can't look at a customer without thinking about how to serve them better and maximize the relationship for mutual growth.

The successful growth of your company starts with the mental keys of commitment and mindset, then proceeds to concrete plans for growth. Setting new targets for growth and performance leads to ideas, strategies, and eventually to tactics that can produce the results you want. As soon as new goals and targets are set, innovation follows to ensure things shift and change to bring the desired results.

Growing a company is not easy and is often the most stressful time for both owners and staff. You are pushing your people, cash flow, and systems to the limit, while having to rebuild and adapt each of them. It's as if your business were an aircraft that takes off while you're still making structural and mechanical changes, until it lands as a superior aircraft. It can be harrowing and challenging for a business, just like for that plane.

Growth is always risky. It seems much safer to play at the level you already know how to manage. Growth requires expansion of skills and abilities. It stretches the boundaries of cash, customer needs, production, and delivery. If you move too fast or too aggressively, you risk taking down your business.

The ideas in this section are keys to managing business growth and performance with more control and awareness. You'll learn how to keep things balanced with a clear vision of how to grow your company and avoid the emotional roller coaster on your way to increased success.

TURNING STONES OF OPPORTUNITY

Business owners often feel pressure to commit to any opportunity that presents itself. Their thinking is influenced by two misguided ideas: 1) this could be *the* opportunity, and 2) another opportunity may never come along again.

The truth is that opportunities are abundant. There is rarely a single opportunity that's the absolute best and most impactful. Opportunities to dramatically grow your company can come frequently and from anywhere, often out of left field.

Opportunities are like stones in a river. You'll pick some up, take a closer look, see how they look underneath, and toss most of them back. You don't wade in and grab the first stone you see. You'll only take a few home, if any at all. In the same way, opportunities need to be considered, then evaluated more closely, and, if possible, tried out to see how they might fit before signing on the dotted line.

As you operate your company, you'll experience a consistent stream of opportunities to consider and evaluate. Opportunities arise across all areas of your business, from production to sales, staffing to technology. You typically won't know which are best until they play themselves out. What appears to be an exceptional opportunity today, could become a total lemon six months from now. So it's important to have a studied approach.

The game of entrepreneurship can require some calculated guesswork and gut checks to determine which opportunities will serve you best. However, the level of risk for some opportunities can be higher than the reward. For example, an innovative change might also have the potential to sink your business. It may not be worth the risk, regardless of how positively it could impact your company.

I know a company that eliminated its entire customer service department and inside sales group. They replaced them with software, a "telephony solution" on the phones, and automated order services on their website. The opportunity screamed of benefits: lower staff costs, faster speed to order, automatic routing into their delivery departments, automatic invoicing, and billing for clients sent immediately by email. But they overlooked the risks. Clients didn't want to complete orders with an automated phone system. Customers didn't want a web page solution. Often, because the products were complex, customers had questions and needed to talk. They'd become used to speaking to their services and sales reps for years, and had relationships with them. Calling was an enjoyable interaction. As sales fell 23 percent in the first year, the company scrambled to recover from their misguided "opportunity."

Part of your role as a striving entrepreneur who wants to grow your business is to actively seek out opportunity. Researching, tracking, and listing ideas should be part of your strategic think time, active routine, and business practice.

Evaluate as many opportunities as you can, be patient and engage only those opportunities that have the most promise and potential to leapfrog your business forward. If you aren't positive about the expected outcomes of an opportunity, then keep researching and evaluating, sample it first, or simply let it go. The river of opportunity has many, many stones for you to turn over.

SYSTEMS NEED TO BE SIMPLE

———

There's a misguided tendency in business to adopt the latest technology and method systems with the idea that they must be better because they're new. Companies jump on the latest ERP software or CRM system regardless of complexity. They decide to systemize production with thirty-one checkpoints and electronic check sheets. They upgrade meeting schedules with thirty-minute video conferences twice daily in an effort to ensure everyone is in the loop all the time.

I used to be trapped in that mindset. I was working in software sales and believed that the key to more sales required the implementation of the latest customer relations management software. I sat beside my old friend Ben who used a pad and pen to track his leads, conversations, and next steps. I'd challenge him that his paper system was antiquated, and my technological advantage would prove more effective in the long run. Ben politely disagreed. Over several months while I was busy syncing versions of my CRM between my computer and server to generate reports, Ben was on the phone with prospective customers.

He knew that his key inputs to sales were personal connections, contacts, and face time. Ben tracked it all in his pad, took notes on every interaction, and kept his data at his fingertips. His methods were simple and time honored; he didn't bother learning new platforms. He led the sales group in performance by following Albert Einstein's advice: "Everything should be made as simple as possible, but not simpler."

Every business function doesn't require a new Excel spreadsheet with macros or a new tracking app. Complicated software, tools, or equipment aren't necessary when simpler systems will get the job done more efficiently. Whenever you look at a new system to support the growth of your business, consider simplicity first and foremost.

When you're considering an upgrade to a new system, be sure to engage the people who'll be using it. For example, a business client of mine spent $40,000 on an online HR system he saw demoed at a conference. He never sought input or discussed it with his HR group. He soon realized that the new software wouldn't work for his team without significant customization that would take up to 400 hours of staff time just to input data. Had he simply consulted his team, he could have saved time and money.

The simpler a system is, the easier it is to engage people. Another past client was looking to invest in Smart whiteboards and cloud-based project management software to manage their design and branding projects. A blank wall, a painted project grid, and Post-it notes became the best system. The group gathered around, talked, updated projects by moving Post-it notes on the wall, and then took action. Meeting time: five to seven minutes. Cost: $25. Simple systems: priceless.

A great rule of thumb is to present the process steps, then ask the persons you're training to repeat them back to you. If they can't repeat it on the first try, then the system needs to be simplified. If a new system is too complicated for the short-term memory capacity of its users, it's bound to fail. This is why it's imperative to consult potential users first, and consider their input before a decision is made to upgrade or improve a system.

KNOW YOUR NUMBERS, METRICS, AND KPIS

———

When your business starts to grow, everything becomes increasingly dynamic. If sales increase, they add pressure to your cash flow, to your staff, your delivery operations, and your costs. It becomes increasingly important to be on top of your key numbers to drive daily performance and manage growth.

Your numbers are not a rough estimate, but exact and specific indicators you can point to in a report. They are some of your most important KPIs, key performance indicators. Great performance and growth are a function of your ability to tightly manage and coordinate your numbers, metrics, and KPIs.

You need to know not only your numbers, but which metrics are the most critical in any situation. So let's take a look at the indicators I've found to be the most relevant overall. Many of them are in constant flux, so look at them regularly in instant summaries on an app, in shared docs stored in the cloud, and in daily, weekly, and monthly reports. They will give you a snapshot of your business every time you review them.

Here are some of my favorite numbers, metrics, and KPIs:

- Sales
  - Total value of the sales pipeline
  - Summary of the weighted sales leads (with likely closing percentage on each sales lead)
  - Top ten prospects per salesperson
  - Value of sales to close in the next thirty days (what are we committing to close this month?)
  - Associated costs of orders the next thirty days (what are we going to need to order?)
- Cash
  - Cash balance
  - Credit balances
  - Accounts receivable total with average days aged
  - Accounts payable total with average days aged
  - Expected cash in the next fifteen and thirty days (as best estimated)
  - Bills to be paid in the next fifteen and thirty days (as best estimated)

- Team
  - Total hours for the last week, fortnight, or month
  - Total labor cost for the last week, fortnight, or month
  - Total overtime hours for the same period
  - Productivity output per shift, per person, per station
- Marketing
  - Total marketing expenses last month
  - Total number of leads generated
  - Cost per lead generated (ROMI)
  - Sales generated from the marketing leads
- Costs
  - Overall cost of goods sold
  - Cost of goods sold per line of sales (if applicable)
  - Gross margin
  - General and administrative costs
  - Random increases in any specific costs

I love to measure and get check-ins on softer numbers and metrics too. For example, the 8+ culture stats of my people (see Secret 43), their feedback on morale, our performance, and their belief in our plan. These aren't daily numbers, but more monthly and quarterly. Just remember: your people are a critical metric that business owners forget to recognize and measure.

Become friendly with the idea of knowing the full measure of your numbers and reviewing them often (some daily, some weekly, and some monthly). Share these with your team so they can participate fully and take responsibility for them too. It's important to remain emotionally neutral with your KPIs and metrics. You can't live and die by every increase or decrease. Metrics give you focus, and tell you what to watch and improve. However, every improvement isn't an occasion for a pizza party, and every setback isn't cause for a staff shakeup.

A manufacturer out of Texas I know uses giant monitors, like sports scoreboards, to post key metrics to their entire team in their 40,000 sq. ft. facility. The sales group can see their hourly sales total, average conversion rate for calls to sales, and week-to-date sales. Production sees their units produced last hour, average number of units per hour, their total output for the week and the total of quality failures. Their team is vividly aware of the numbers that determine their success. They always know the score in their game.

If you aren't monitoring your numbers and metrics now, start with just a handful, three to five to begin with. Don't try to begin reporting on twenty metrics and numbers all at once. Start with simple ones like daily sales and daily labor costs. Open discussions with your team about these numbers and get their feedback. You'll soon start to see trends, and within a short period, you'll know what your numbers are telling you about how to manage your business' progress and growth. You'll find out what it means to really "know your numbers."

+1 EFFECT

———

You may be hoping for the one client account that changes everything in your sales and cash flow. You may be looking for a revolution in manufacturing that suddenly improves the overall performance of your operations. Neither is likely to happen overnight. For business owners and entrepreneurs, improvements come as small gains and innovations. Incremental changes are the keys to your success in business.

You can be open to big change, but in the meantime stay busy pushing for small improvements every day. With every change I make, I am looking for a 1 percent, one second, or $1 improvement. My team and I are always pushing ourselves to make simple, incremental improvements, so it never seems overwhelming or unreachable. When companies set expectations for overwhelming change, they inadvertently erect barriers to smaller levels of improvement that would be more attainable. It's far more productive to pursue achievable advances that people can believe are possible and can be completed quickly. I call it the +1 Effect.

You and your team can regularly be celebrating small gains and wins that lift everyone's pride and performance. With a +1 Effect, expectations for incremental betterment are attainable, and a rhythm is set for success in smaller stages of growth. It's a version of what's called *kaizen* culture in Japan, which translates as constant, never-ending improvement.

One of the best examples of the +1 Effect at work occurred in my friend Jerry's print shop. Since opening his business, Jerry hadn't consistently hit daily break-even sales. In fact, he often lost some money each day, so his operation was falling short of being profitable.

Jerry brought me in as an advisor and business coach. The first thing I asked him was whether his team knew what the break-even figure was for business daily. He told me they didn't, and that he was afraid to share it with them. So we sat down with the entire staff and explained that they had a goal of sales to reach each day. That goal allowed everyone to get paid, to pay all the bills on time, to leave a little extra to build a reserve of cash for emergencies and for future growth of the business.

Staff often think that increased sales just puts money in the pocket of the owner. Therefore it was important for them to know what was really at stake where they worked. They needed to understand why a healthy level of business was vital for everyone involved to succeed. The business' daily costs were about $1,100, so we started by creating a small, achievable buffer of $100 above those costs. The only change we made was to set that goal for the team. Within ten days, the staff moved the business from an average of $1,015 a day in sales to an average of $1,262. We shared the sales progress a few times each day, so they knew when they were on track. The dynamic we created was enough motivation for the staff to intuitively change how they approached their work activities and interactions with customers to manage their daily success.

We gathered the team and told them how fantastic they were doing, and shared the numbers with them. Then we said, we'd like to move the sales goal to $1,325 a day. Within weeks they were hitting the new sales number. Then we set the target just a little higher to $1,450, a goal that we thought was still reachable. Each time, the team adjusted their efforts and methods to raise sales without any special training or substantial alteration to the business. Why did the team work so hard to achieve the goal? Because people inherently want to contribute and succeed!

This went on for about five months until the business was doing around $1,475 a day. Jerry's business was now healthy and profitable with an upbeat culture of performance.

This same approach can be used in any aspect of a business, not just financial. It involves four basic steps:

1. Sharing the existing performance
2. Setting a new marginally higher level of performance (with an explanation of *why* this is important)
3. Measuring the gains
4. Celebrating the success with everyone

Like a track star trying to shave just a few hundredths of a second off their time, you can grow and master your business with regular, small improvements across the board.

SECRET 82

FIRE CLIENTS REGULARLY

———

Firing clients is a good thing. I know it's counterintuitive, but it's true. Firing clients is a critical step to improving performance and growth. Old clients often hold expectations from an older version of your business. They are the ones who can keep you from innovating and improving because they are tied to the old pricing, the old process, and the old timing of your business.

The tendency when starting out in business is to accept anyone as a client. It's understandable. New businesses are desperate to succeed and will take on anyone who's willing to pay. If they're slow to pay, you accept it. If they ask for special deals, you'll try to make it happen, even if you'd rather not.

Eventually your business gets busy enough that these

older clients with all their old expectations start to drive you crazy. By this time, you've learned what makes a better client. You've become increasingly aware of how high maintenance your older customers are, and how unprofitable they have turned out to be. Your new customers are the kind who are attracted to your new business model. So, you try to shift your older clients over to your new way of doing things, but you're met with resistance.

Eventually you reach a breaking point. It's time to release them to go find another supplier, which is a nice way of saying, you fire them. And that's good news. By setting them free, you free yourself to conduct business in the way you prefer. As you raise the offerings of your company through better products and service delivery, and different pricing, you'll find a match with better customers. Letting go of old habits with problem clients is how you create space for newer clients. Older, incompatible clients take up your time and stall your progress. Get comfortable knowing that to grow and improve your business performance, some clients just won't travel with you. However, a few will. Some clients will love you and your business enough to make the changes necessary to stay with you.

My good friend and personal trainer, Ron Jarrett, moved gyms four times before opening his own, which forced me to move with him. His rates have gone up, his schedule is tight, and he's in high demand. As a client, I made the decision over and over to adapt and follow him, because he's that good. Ron will tell you that with each move and change in his operations he lost clients, but they were mostly the ones who didn't match his new offerings.

How do you get used to the idea of firing a client? Simple. Think of just one client, the one who doesn't pay and complains about every delivery or product they receive. That's where you start, because it's going to feel really good to let that client go. Your staff will thank you, because they know the bad clients as well as you do. Let your soon-to-be-ex-client know that you no longer think it's a good fit to continue doing business. Recommend them to someone else in the industry who will fit their needs better.

Firing clients will empower you to manage your customer base. It will give you control over client performance and symmetry to grow your business faster.

CREATE THE DESIRED EXPERIENCE

———

Life is a series of experiences, many of them emotional. We remember the first time we rode a bike, our first day of school, our first date. Hopefully our experiences are pleasant ones, but of course they can't all be. Your business is a series of emotional experiences too, for you, your customers, and staff. The question is: are those experiences pleasant or unpleasant? Successful businesses are highly effective at creating the desired experience for the people they serve.

In retail and service industries—clothing stores, restaurants, hotels, spas—it's easier to gauge the quality of customer experience. Interactions are easier to see, customer engagement is upfront and close. But what if your business is a machine shop? What if you're a warehousing operation? It can be more challenging to identify the touchpoints of your clients' experience and create the experience they desire.

As an example, let's look at an industry that's infamous for creating "less than satisfying" customer experiences: your neighborhood mechanic. You go into the front office, which is outdated, dirty, and smells of motor oil. There are two worn-out chairs and a small table with decade-old magazines, many of which are inappropriate for a place of business. The guy who comes out to serve you says, "Yeah?" You explain the problem that needs fixing and that you have an appointment. He takes your keys and phone number, but gives no indication of when they'll call or what he thinks might be causing the mechanical problem. You call Uber or a cab and go back home or to work. That's your underwhelming experience of dropping off your car for repair.

Now contrast that with an auto repair shop that values customer experience. Fresh coffee is brewing in the waiting area for customers and the team, comfortable chairs are available along with recent magazines, and music is playing in the work area at a reasonable volume. A service manager or the owner talks with you about the car problem, offers to call a cab, and gives an approximate time of when they'll call with a diagnosis. During that call they'll explain the work that's necessary, the parts needed, how long it will take, and the approximate cost. When the work is completed, you are shown the old parts, the repair is explained in more detail, and the receipt shows the tally of time and parts. When your car is pulled around front, it has also been washed and it's glowing.

The experience is entirely different, you leave satisfied, and the shop has earned your loyalty and repeat business. Any business can provide customers with their desired experience. It is about simply the commitment and desire to offer more. It's the absolute winning method for growth and longevity in any industry.

Delivering the desired experience is not all that complicated. Start by making a list of items you can improve to raise the bar of customer service and interaction. Get your staff involved in defining that experience. Brainstorm everything the team can do, no matter how outrageous, then select the best ideas and start to implement them. See how they work out. What works best can then be systemized into a series of precise steps that become the standard for consistency in your business process.

Start with what you can do for free, then be generous with added-cost ideas. Expect to spend a little money on improvement; it's well worth it. The added costs for delivering great experiences to your customers and staff will be recaptured in increased business, as well as small price increases that your customers won't even notice, or will gladly pay for the service they receive.

For years friends and I went on an annual NFL boys' weekend. We always chose the hotel chain that offered the warm chocolate chip cookies when we checked in. We'd spend thousands on hotel rooms based on $10 worth of cookies.

Make your business an experience everyone appreciates and brags about to others. Exceptional service experiences replace expensive marketing as the key to driving more business.

CRITICAL NON-ESSENTIALS

———

Paddi Lund is a dentist in Australia who has transformed his dental experience from something his patients once dreaded to something they actually look forward to. He hasn't revolutionized dental techniques, but rather the experience itself, the small details and delivery of dental service to his patients. In his own unique way, Paddi has changed dentistry with what he calls Critical Non-Essentials (CNEs).

What Paddi has done is isolate critical pieces of service delivery outside the usual practice of dentistry. CNEs are so important in distinguishing a business because, for most of us, our core service or product is basically the same as what our competitors offer. Customers generally don't see much variation between your product and that of your competition. This is why so many people use price as the primary determining factor in their buying choices. When a product or service is basically the same, a buyer will simply go for the lowest cost. This is where Critical Non-Essentials can bend the curve in your direction.

As described in Secret 6, Paddi centered his practice on hospitality, offering great espresso, eighty types of tea, and little pastries called Dental Buns. His office provides service with a smile, and the smiles and attitude are infectious. People love being at his dental office. His practice has become so busy that he has a long waiting list of referrals. Paddi recognized that so much of his business could be developed outside of the actual service he offers when people are in the dental chair. He has mastered all of the critical services that make his business different, and yet they are not the essential service of dentistry.

Clients judge a service or product on the overall experience, not only by how well a product serves their needs, but by how friendly the staff are at a restaurant or the smile of a cashier at the supermarket. A customer's criteria may have little to do with the core service, but everything to do with Critical Non-Essentials, such as whether a lawyer's office calls you back quickly with a response time guarantee, the free mini cookies for kids at a bakery, or flowers for a year from the realtor who helped you buy a home.

Sometimes, in order to give your clients more, you need

to raise your prices by 2 to 5 percent. This can give you enough margin to budget for customer treats, free bottled water, giveaway swag, or the hiring of extra staff. You might also want to invest in software to track customer purchase history and product preferences, those essential details that can make all the difference in meeting customer needs. Customers won't notice the price change, but they will notice the improvements you've made with CNEs. They will *feel* the difference, and you will too.

OUTGROW EVERYTHING

To maximize the growth of your business, you need to assume that your business will outgrow everything you have in place now. As your business progresses, you will outgrow old processes, supports, customers, and suppliers. Obvious signs of growth are adding more staff, more clients, and other product lines.

If you have advisors, they may be effective at your current level, but perhaps not into the future. As your business grows, you may need to find advisors with broader experience in your industry. For example, your accountant, lawyer, or business coach may not be up to the scope and complexity of the changes you need to make. It's important to have healthy caution about the advice you get, and to double-check it with other sources. Misinformed advice can delay or cause serious damage to your growth and performance.

Your existing customers won't all transition through the growth with you. The changes you make to your services, products, and pricing may not appeal to all of your present clients and vendors. For example, a grocery store that delivers to their best customers may find over time that personal deliveries are no longer an option. In-store sales have grown and deliveries have become too time-consuming to handle. It's just a natural evolution.

The staff you have may not be able to transition into the future roles you need to fill. Your bookkeeper may not have the skills to assume the responsibilities of a financial controller. Your hands-on production manager may not be equipped to be a general manager. Your prep cook may not transition to a solid sous chef. You must evaluate everyone who shows potential. Part of your responsibility will be to upskill existing staff, and prepare them for the coming roles business growth demands. Always make mental notes of the people you believe can grow and respond with advanced skills and talents as your business grows and changes. Challenge them to step up to new business needs, and show them how it will be to their benefit. Build growth into your company culture and prepare your team for opportunities that lie ahead.

Your systems and processes will need to adapt to change. What worked for producing one hundred widgets a week, will need to evolve in order to produce 1,000 widgets.

Your customer service decisions will need to be formalized as policies your client-facing staff can reference. They need to be able to handle customer service without asking for advice whenever a situation arises. This will prevent a significant bottleneck in your operations.

You will likely outgrow your facilities or office space. For example, a couple I know started an online business in their home. They were selling GPS devices online, and soon the entire house and garage were full of inventory. They moved into a small retail office and warehouse, but as the business continued to expand, they outgrew that space too. Keep in mind that moving disrupts operations, so it's always wise to plan ahead for growth.

When selecting a new space, make sure that it's large enough for continued growth, but not too large. I know an advertising agency that went from 3,500 sq. ft. to over 18,000 sq. ft. in office space. What they needed was about 6,000 sq. ft. for their team, and they hoped they'd grow into the extra area over time (hope being the treacherous term). But their new lease costs started to kill them, and their profits as well. Their efforts toward growth and increased sales had to take a backseat to sub-leasing some of their space just to cover rent. During times of big expansion, avoid locking yourself into a restricted location for too long. It's best to keep leases short so that transition is flexible.

One of the most successful entrepreneurs I know has been buying franchises for the last fifteen years. Dave's secret is his appreciation for how systemized a franchise is from day one. He makes certain that the franchises he buys have stress-tested their systems and processes for successful business operations. He knows his key role is to drive sales, so he constantly looks for the next aspects of a business that need upgrading based on sales growth. He proactively watches for what needs to improve in the coming quarter, six months, and year. He adapts for growth ahead of time and plans effectively every step of the way.

High-growth periods force you to become comfortable with disrupting current standards. Everything will change at a fast pace. What you once saw as fixed and certain can't remain the same. You need to be prepared to make tough decisions, evaluate everything, and guide your team through the dynamic flux of your business.

Be aware, however, that continued growth at all costs is not effective. Even fast-growth companies need to consciously take time off from perpetual, massive growth. This could entail waiting a month before launching the next product innovation or marketing campaign, or taking a summer hiatus from pursuing new sales channels. It can be productive to take a few days, weeks, or months to stop and settle into new changes. Stop the growth push long enough to recharge your staff, and yourself, before you push for more again. Outgrowing everything is the long-term plan, but it doesn't mean that growth can't coexist with a pace that keeps the company enjoyable and energizing.

BUILD COMMUNITY

———

The best businesses I've been involved in are companies that build strong communities. For example, I started two music venues with my business partner, Soren, to showcase great blues and roots music. It wasn't even my type of music when we started, but it soon became a passion of mine. I became immersed in the communities that surrounded the artists. Our clubs were places where people came to eat, drink, listen to live music, and socialize with other music fans. We tapped into a community of people with shared musical passions and built our business right along with them.

This community of music fans supported our vision and enterprise in more ways than just attending performances and spending their money. They planned social events at our club, they volunteered for us, and even helped us renovate our second music venue for free! They were a group of people that wanted to see us succeed. They were invested in our music community and wanted us to thrive as much as we did. We needed each other, and that need drove a symbiotic relationship around music for years.

Creating a community around an entertainment venue might seem easy compared to the nature of your business. However, people jump on board and create communities around everything from Harley-Davidson motorcycles to Lululemon yoga gear to tech platforms such as Apple, or the places they shop for food, such as Whole Foods or Community Foods (community is in the name!).

Building a community goes beyond just delivering your services or product. Building community means getting to know your clients and bringing them together. As clients form relationships around your business, a community naturally emerges. Your job is to make sure that your business and your communications become the driving force of your community. Think of it like a Facebook group: you set up the group, feed the group with messaging, direction, and content such as videos. Soon other users in the group start to share, interact, and take the group in directions you hadn't expected. You continue to duck into the group regularly, but your input is now only a portion of the activity and interaction taking place. This is a creation model for any community, whether online or in the physical world.

Creating a community involves caring. As a business,

people need to know that you care about more than just sales. They want to know that the community itself and the people who are part of it really mean something to you. They can read your motivations. People will very quickly sense your driving force. They can spot the difference between a promotion and a real contribution of your time, resources, and team. If you sponsor a kids' football team, do it because you love the sport and the kids. Soon parents and coaches will be supporting your business too. That's the order in which it works. Caring comes first.

I can tell you full stop that building a community feels great. It satisfies the needs of an entrepreneur beyond just business numbers. It feels good to know you're bringing people together for shared interests and passions. Add community to the vision for your company and watch your business improve and grow in performance and satisfaction.

THREE LEVELS OF PROSPECTS

———

Occasionally you hear about some company that landed a massive contract that virtually blew up the company's sales and size overnight. They went from $100,000 to $30,000,000 almost instantly. Treat these stories like a unicorn sighting—rare and tough to verify. Sure, it's possible you'll be the next company to land a client that increases your sales by 3,000 percent. Being hit by lightning is also a possibility.

Instead of hoping for the unicorn of opportunity and big sales to land on you, build a growth plan that maximizes your prospects in the marketplace. In each market, there are golden prospects and clients to work with: high margin, good people, with large ongoing orders. There are also far more not-so-golden clients you're better off to avoid: small orders with lots of demands and infrequent purchases that are slow to pay. Develop a profile of these different prospective clients and put them in a database. Get to know the companies and the people you prefer to do business with.

At my companies, we typically break down prospects into three groups:

1. Thanks, No Thanks prospects
2. Oxygen accounts
3. Dream accounts

I've also seen these groups described as fish: minnows, salmon, and whales. This division of prospects into levels is not new. What is new is the time allocation I recommend spending on each group.

Traditionally, companies spend incorrect amounts of time with the Thanks, No Thanks size clients, where there is a lot of work for limited profits and cash, but sales can be plentiful and immediate. The accounts that are the building blocks of a business, the Oxygen prospects, are often dabbled in, but not with the focus they really need. Dream accounts, where it could take years to close an account, and where there are many sales variables outside your control, are often too large a focus, which puts sales at risk if something goes wrong, or they are ignored as not being viable opportunities.

For example, a client of ours sells chemicals to manufacturing companies. When we began consulting with them, they had a handful of significant Dream accounts around the country in the range of $100,000 to $500,000 in annual sales value. They had a lot of midsized, Oxygen accounts in the $10,000 to $100,000 range. Finally, there were the Thanks, No Thanks small shops that might make a purchase of $500 to $10,000 once a year, or request so little product that shipping costs were more than the order. The sales team of young, talented, and capable people were getting decent results, but their focus was wrong.

Here's how they were splitting their time:

- Thanks, No Thanks accounts: 60 percent
- Oxygen accounts: 35 percent
- Dream accounts: 5 percent

Given the percentages, we realized that it was the Dream accounts that could dramatically impact sales and add to growth. Yet there was minimal time focused on approaching those accounts. Keep in mind that I don't usually recommend increased focus on Dream accounts first, but in this case they'd already made Oxygen accounts a decent focus. At this company, however, the balance was off with only 5 percent focus on Dream accounts, too much emphasis at 60 percent on Thanks, No Thanks accounts, while Oxygen accounts were better, but still low at 35 percent. So we decided to shift the focus of the sales team to be more efficient and effective. We mapped each Dream account with actions to move that account forward. We determined what offers the sales team could make and how they could build a relationship with each Dream prospect. We coached them in all the small actions they could take over time toward landing those Dream accounts. We expected the sales cycles to be six to eighteen months before the team really got to sell their products.

Next we looked at the clients the sales team needed to interact with less often. The Thanks, No Thanks clients often took a lot of time to service, but really only needed administrative help to make reorders and to discuss issues around price and shipping logistics. We agreed that simply letting some of these clients go was a calculated risk. The admin staff would start to handle these orders and clients directly. If these customers left, it was okay because the loss in sales would be offset by the free time created for the sales team to go after the good clients.

We moved the time and focus allocation of the salespeople to new percentages of emphasis:

- Thanks, No Thanks accounts: 10 percent (from 60) = less emphasis

- Oxygen accounts: 60 percent (from 35) = more emphasis
- Dream accounts: 30 percent (from 5) = more emphasis

The impact on sales didn't change overnight, but we soon started to see the number of Dream accounts that were active move from three to eleven. We saw sales start to increase steadily month after month, year over year, with better sales from the Oxygen accounts, which were faster to close and still large enough to really impact the monthly sales totals. In the last sixteen months, eight of them have been new monthly sales records. Oxygen accounts continue to order more, and Dream accounts are now lined up to drive up future sales by 20 to 30 percent. The size of the sales team has now doubled, providing better customer service too. And, ironically, the Thanks, No Thanks clients have also stuck around with only a few exceptions. The admin team manages them day-to-day.

The upshot is this: Determine the categories and profiles of your prospective clients. Then break down the time and energy focus for each group with your team. Make those Oxygen accounts your daily priority. Give Dream accounts small actions consistently to move them forward. Move your Thanks, No Thanks clients to your admin team and to support people outside your sales team. Do these things and your sales over the next six to eighteen months will jump. Your salespeople will have more fun because sales will be a game people want to dive into with renewed focus and results.

HELP FROM GROWTH PARTNERS

Fierce independence can be a helpful attribute for an entrepreneur. It allows for the ability to see things that others are blind to, and it fuels the creativity and persistence of business visionaries. That fierce independence is what compels entrepreneurship, but it can also be a curse once a company is beyond the start-up phase, because growing a company is something you can't do alone.

Once you have a company stabilized with a team, customers, and processes in place, your focus becomes scaling and growing your business. To grow a company dramatically requires a new focus of leverage and growth by multiples (the popular 10X viewpoint). For example, an IT hardware company that sets up IT infrastructure in new office spaces, needs to know which companies are relocating, starting up, or opening new branch offices. Leverage means getting to know commercial real estate brokers who are filling many of those office spaces, and contractors who are renovating those spaces for new tenants. The IT firm needs to be in the loop to pick up work on an ongoing basis. This is why companies form alliances and partnerships that are mutually beneficial for business expansion.

Who can you leverage to take your company to the next level? Who can deliver leads to you almost daily? Which companies can help you take your business national or global? It's crucial to connect to the networks, organizations, and people who can broaden your market. As you form and establish your company, stay keenly aware of contacts and keep expanding your list of acquaintances and associates, suppliers, vendors, and marketing specialists who would be ideal to help promote your product or to offer referrals.

For example, a software company that develops a great reporting tool for sales data should consider contacting Salesforce.com as a number one target for partnering and growth. Salesforce could introduce their reporting platform as an extension of the internal reporting that Salesforce already provides. This would instantly open up the company's product to millions of users. Oprah's Favorite Things episodes launched many companies into the stratosphere of sales simply by her profiling and endorsing their products.

Putting promotional deals together can take a long time, and it can be intimidating to approach the "big fish," so most people don't. They look to see who can help them in their local market and only dabble at the fringes. My recommendation is to be open to both big and small leads. Local contacts can help you grow, but don't shy away from game-changing alliances in the big leagues that can transform your company.

Every entrepreneur should keep a business planning journal or an "ideas book," either digitally or on paper. Devote a section to connections in your current market and beyond. Who are the people and companies you'd most like to partner with for mutual promotion? Also keep a dream list of trendsetters and influential companies you'd like to reach out to. Add people to the list boldly, no matter what level of success or celebrity they might have.

Strive for twenty connections to consider and pursue. Start with those who are easiest to approach and work your way up. See what kind of feedback you get. You need to pitch your idea a few times to see how it works and where it fails. Adapt and make changes for how to best position your product or service and improve your pitch.

One connection leads to another as people make referrals and introduce you to other people they know. Your LinkedIn contacts expand and your name starts getting around. Your exposure on social media grows and people start reaching out to you. Before you know it, you're bookending meetings with new acquaintances. Some will fizzle, but others will become long-term opportunities to leverage your company in broader markets and with partners who are excited about your company and its potential in the wider marketplace.

Over the years, I've talked to media people in television and the recording industry, executives of airlines and national food brands, and leaders of global companies. At times, I must admit, I've sometimes been too intimidated to pursue connections I feared were out of my league. I've had Bill Gates' cell number for years and never called. But that's okay. Reaching out to people to help grow your company is a muscle you need to flex and strengthen. It grows with time and you always get better at it.

Approach people with the kind of enthusiasm that says your product or service is a game changer. Lead with your understanding of how your product or service is valuable to them. Your courage to connect beyond your comfort zone will take you places you never imagined. It will help your company grow incrementally and expand your playing field. You may very well have the right big idea at the right moment in time, but you'll never know its potential unless you continually work to leverage and grow your partner network.

CLOSEST TO THE MONEY

———

Growing your business involves many moving parts. It's a daunting process, and my advice is to focus on the money. Cash is the lifeblood of your business, so push away all the other noise. Work with your team to concentrate on activities associated with cash and sales. I call this system my Four Ps of Closest to the Money:

1. Payment
2. Paper
3. People
4. Process

Start each day with *payment*. Ask, "Where can we collect cash? Where can we process a credit card, or pick up a check? Which clients on our accounts receivable list can we call to organize a payment today?"

The bull's-eye of the Closest to the Money target is anything you can do today to actually get a payment and put money into your bank account. People have asked me, "Is getting in the car and driving across town to pick up a check the best use of my time?" In short, yes. Collecting payments is the lifeblood and the most valuable action of your business. It should be part of your company culture. Would I drive across town for $5? Most likely not, it isn't worth my time, or yours. But I'd get a credit card number over the phone and process that $5 today.

Once I've looked at all the sources of immediate payment, I go to the next circle in my Closest to the Money target, which is *paper*. Where can I write a contract? Where can I generate an invoice? Who needs a quote? These are the paper items that will result in payments in the coming days and weeks. Most salespeople have prospective customers they have emailed an agreement for signature, but it hasn't been completed. Get them on the phone or drive over, go through the agreement and get it signed now! Go through your orders and client base, decide who to send an invoice for services, product, work in progress, or a deposit. By focusing on paper items now, you are looking ahead to next week's cash, and this should drive the urgency for you and your team.

Once these first two levels of payment and paper have been executed, I look to the next circle, which is *people*. Who are the people you can connect with to do business today? This could be sales meetings, new prospecting meetings, networking functions, or supplier meetings. It is any in-person meeting or phone call that can result in potentially doing business today or in the near future. It is not emails. Only live conversation truly moves business forward. An email is too easy to ignore or misplace in the vast sea of emails, and too hard to evaluate: "I think they liked it and might sign," means you aren't really sure and aren't in control.

Finally, I look at the fourth circle in the Closest to the Money target: *process*. What process do we need to change or improve to generate more cash? This is the last place of focus because changing a process takes time, and the results are usually delayed.

For example, marketing is a process. Even if you start fleshing out a campaign idea today, it can take weeks to create the materials and ads. Then you need to test the results and potentially tweak and change your campaign. Months from now, it might be starting to work and generating leads.

Changes to your sales process also takes time to generate measurable results. It is worth doing, just not the first place to start. The same holds true for reviewing inventory levels and your process for managing inventory. Changes related to customer experience are also changes in process, and can be worth the time and consideration, but are not the place to start. Changes in process can potentially free up cash in the future, but not as fast as selling something today or collecting payments.

Businesses demand cash to fund their growth. Therefore start each day looking at the Closest to the Money target of payments, paper, people, and then process. Use this tiered structure as a guide for where to focus your team's attention for steady cash flow.

SECRET 90

REPEAT BUSINESS

───

Most people don't have a love for multi-level marketing (MLM) companies. We've all dealt with them in one form or another: a friend or acquaintance organizes a candle party, or they're pitching health and beauty products, or juice extracts or vitamins; a telecom company offers to save you money for each friend or neighbor you recruit to their service. The pressure to sell to the people you know makes the business model a real challenge in the long term.

It's a dubious enterprise for the customer/distributor, but the MLM industry knows that the secret to growth is getting their client base and downline distributors using the product daily and weekly. Products are packaged to last a week and are sold in volumes that run out monthly. That's the way sales and consumption in the MLM market are designed. They calculate usage on a standard schedule of biweekly payments to ensure constant, uninterrupted cash flow like clockwork.

What this shows is that repeat sales is a key to growing your company indefinitely. Your goal is to get your customers buying on a consistent basis. Client dependency on your product or service is a good thing to strive for as a business owner. You need to design your business beyond single-customer transactions.

But what if your business is really based on a one-time purchase? In that case, you need to get creative in finding continued sales add-ons. Here are just a few:

- Furniture sales: corporate storage, reupholstery, cleaning
- Home construction: annual maintenance or renovation packages
- Massage: monthly membership instead of single appointments
- Websites: annual refresh package, SEO programs, content campaigns

Add-on packages can shift the overall focus on your business. There are options for every company. Over time, add-on products and services can become a larger component of the company's revenue than the original sale item. In this way, value increases for both the company and the customer. The company receives recurring revenue and the customer receives ongoing service and a need always fulfilled.

The best way to discover what kind of added, regular services you can offer is to ask your customers. When IKEA asked customers what issues, if any, came up with their purchases, the company learned what a headache it was for buyers to tie boxes to the roofs of their cars. After bringing their purchases home, customers had problems trying to assemble furniture that was supposed to take an hour, but took six! So IKEA added tie-down materials to their loading areas and crews to deliver and assemble furniture on-site at customers' homes. In doing so, they added new revenue streams to their business model.

Find out what supporting product line or service will serve your customers. Several years ago, I had a client who sold silk plants. The business had cans of spray cleaner in their inventory, but seldom sold any of it. The plants were a one-time purchase, so we decided that every sale was an add-on opportunity for this "miracle" cleaner that actually made dust and dirt on silk plants disappear (I still don't know how). The combined sales of plants and cleaner increased the company's margins overall. Customers got hooked on the product, and sales of spray cleaner increased steadily as people came back for more. This one change increased profits to the extent that the business owners had all of their vacations paid for annually by spray cleaner!

Start thinking of a lifetime relationship with your customers. What are they going to need beyond your core, one-time purchased product? What other items or services can you give to them that they will gladly use far into the future? Be like the landscaper who plants trees, prunes them seasonally, removes old ones, and plants new ones again. In every business there is a life cycle you can tap into for greater long-term service and sales growth.

PART NINE

OWNER MANAGEMENT: YES, MANAGING YOURSELF

The biggest asset to your business is you. The biggest hindrance to your business is also you. It works this way because the owner or entrepreneur is the single most significant and influential force in a company.

Being an entrepreneur demands more energy, time, and skills than any other job. It means knowing all aspects of the business from marketing to sales, operations to finance, planning to administration, and team management to business strategy. Being an entrepreneur demands that you consistently raise your game, and ultimately find a way to manage yourself.

Self-management requires strong self-awareness. It requires honest recognition of what you do well and what you need to do better. A strong entrepreneur knows their personal scorecard and has a good understanding of their limits, and how those limits can affect the business. This allows for correct decision-making and delegation of responsibility, to see where opportunities lie and how to use the team to reach them.

Self-management is something entrepreneurs rarely discuss and few practice well. An entrepreneur who is keenly self-aware doesn't let personal needs or ego come before the needs of the business, the team, and customers. Owners who are disciplined in self-management practice appropriate work/life balance and see to it that their staff do also. Many business owners and entrepreneurs wear life imbalance, and incredibly long hours, as badges of accomplishment. Long-term business sustainability and success demand that the business owner recognize the physical, emotional, and spiritual needs that inform the direction, focus, energy, and drive of an organization.

As anyone who's flown on a commercial jet knows, in order to help others in an emergency, you need to put your own oxygen mask on first. The entrepreneur therefore needs to work on himself or herself first, each and every day. Small improvements in your mindset, habits, and knowledge lead to long-term improvements in your company. You need to stay sharp, focused, and energized to guide, grow, and, sustain your organization. Success begins with self-management.

STOP BEING THE NUCLEUS

If you need to be the key decision-maker, information holder, and authority in your business, you unequivocally restrict the potential of your company. Only by empowering your people to make decisions and operate with some degree of autonomy can you empower your business. It's a hard lesson to learn, but business owners need to stop being the absolute nucleus of their companies.

An owner's need for control is understandable. When you started your business, it was all you: the concept, the vision, and the risk. But there comes a time when the entrepreneur's control needs to give way to a new structure of organized delegation and reporting.

It's important, of course, that you understand each component of your company before you hand it off. Once you have a working knowledge of a particular aspect of the company, hand off the responsibility, determine the key information you need back, and design the reporting system. Test it to see if it works for team members and yourself. It may need some tweaks, then hand it off again.

Understand, however, that delegating authority doesn't mean you simply walk away from overall responsibility and planning. When a business owner hires a controller, financial reporting still goes to the owner. Entrepreneurs keep duly informed of how sales are trending and where resources are being spent, cash in and cash out, with a sharp eye on quarterly earnings and profit. It's all necessary for planning both short term and long term.

By effectively handing off authority, the business owner frees time for growth and strategic planning, positioning the company for innovation and changes in the marketplace. Forward-thinking owners train their teams to decide and execute on the microscale, and create a feedback loop of sharing critical information necessary for planning on the macroscale. The entrepreneur receives daily and weekly updates, monthly and quarterly reports, and summaries for the widest application of knowledge to drive the company toward growth. This is infinitely more effective for the owner and the entire organization.

I knew a retail entrepreneur who operated twenty-one

liquor stores. He told me he worked about three hours a day on them. When I asked him how he did it, he told me that every store had to provide him with their daily report by 9 a.m. the next morning. He sat down with his coffee and reviewed those reports for sales, inventory levels, staff hours, products to order, and notes on any issues. In a single page, he could get a snapshot of the whole business. Over time, as he became more adept at reading the numbers, he could instantly see when something was off and if he needed to check into it. That meant a phone call or sometimes a trip to a store. Even with this follow-up, he was done working by noon. When traveling, he could go through the same process on his smartphone. He reviewed reports, sent emails and text messages, and continued his travels and vacations.

Every business owner needs to move from doing everything and being the nucleus of control to becoming the all-knowing hub of the wheel. As the hub, you get the information and are removed from the action of the wheel spinning around you. This is the critical position for empowering your spokes (your people) and scaling your company. Your people will appreciate the responsibility and trust you place in them, and will love you for it.

Start by making a list of all the things you control today. Then begin to hand off each of those responsibilities one at a time. Give your team the information they'll need to deliver on those responsibilities, train them on the process, and explain the information you need back. You'll be shocked at how fast and effectively you can release control.

You can always dive back into any area of your company, when you like. Go visit production, drive a forklift, take customer orders. Only now, you won't be trapped in that operational role and restricting your company's growth into the future.

MANAGE YOUR TIME

I have a best friend Dean who moved down to Santa Clara, California, to work in the tech sector as Silicon Valley really took off. He excelled as a programmer, and began to get promotions until he became a manager and then a director of people. He spent his whole day answering questions and fixing problems. He told me, "I can't even start my own work until three or four in the afternoon!"

"Welcome to management," I said.

Managing your business has a cost: your time. For most entrepreneurs concerned with their team, their customers, and their suppliers and vendors, the attention you provide to these people eats up your time.

Business owners aren't working sixty and seventy hours a week on their own projects. They are helping others for fifty of those hours, and trying to squeeze another ten or twenty for their own work in the early morning or late at night. For the average entrepreneur, the day starts to get away from them as soon as the first person shows up for work. Frustrated owners are always telling me there's a lineup of people at their office door needing to ask questions. You'd think they were a country's president or prime minister with a new agenda item scheduled every ten minutes.

So, starting right now, begin valuing your time as though you were the president of your own country. This means that no one sees you without an appointment. Staff can't just barge in. Have someone guard your calendar and hold your time sacred. You are too busy running a country called Your Company to deal with every issue of every citizen who comes knocking at your door.

If you think that by making yourself freely available to staff, customers, and suppliers all day long, you are serving them effectively, you're not. The path to success is *not* complete availability. It's far more productive for you, your company, staff, and clients to be managing your time correctly.

Here's how to get started on effective time self-management:

- Know the tasks and the severity of issues you need

to weigh in on, and which ones you can allow your team to deal with.

- Set blocks of time in your calendar for personal work time. I recommend leaving the office and fulfilling this work time from a home office or a third space, such as a coffee shop where you can relax and concentrate.
- Lock your office door. It's the most effective tool to get people to stop interrupting you. An owner once told me, "But they'll keep knocking if they know I'm in there." Trust me, people will only knock for about three minutes before their arm and brain tells them to stop. In any given hour, that leaves you fifty-seven minutes to still work quietly.
- Buy some good Bose, Beats, or other sound-canceling headphones. Having worked in the same direct space as my assistant, I found that headphones do two things: they signal that I'm focused and working, and they eliminate any noise (including other voices) that can distract me.
- Set office hours. It works for college professors and it will work for you too. Let staff know you'll be available for questions and fifteen-minute meetings between 10 and 11:30 a.m. each day. Have them sign up on a board outside your office. It might sound crazy to restrict your time like this, but if people have to sign up in advance for a time slot, it ensures they'll take your time more seriously.

- Have someone else control your calendar. No one is more effective at keeping strict rules about your time than someone who is assigned to the task. I break my calendar rules far more often than my assistant ever will. She knows and respects the value of my time much more than I do. She tells people "no" when they ask for five unscheduled minutes, but gladly books them on my calendar for a future date.

You cannot effectively build a company if you are a slave to the people in that company. No president could run a country effectively if every citizen, politician, and foreign dignitary had free access. Stop believing that being available to people is serving them.

If you value your time and see it as critically important to your role as a business leader, others will too. They will accept it because it makes sense, and they'll respect you more for it. It will also empower them to be more efficient and responsible with their own time.

DECISIONS—MAKE THEM FAST

———

Momentum is essential in business. You've probably felt it in sales when everything seems to be rolling, and orders are coming in effortlessly. You've probably also felt the opposite, when you're doing the work, trying everything you can think of, and nothing seems to be selling or working for you.

Momentum is either there or it isn't. One of the keys to making sure it *is* there involves fast decision-making. The opposite is also true: dragging your feet will slow your company's momentum. I'm not advocating snap decisions on everything. It's not like the "speed round" on a game show with your hair-trigger finger on a buzzer. It's about the effectiveness of timely and regular decisions that keep innovation and operations progressing.

Indecision hampers your business growth. Staff members of a struggling company often know what they want to happen, they know what needs to be done, but they are left waiting while owners or managers deliberate. Frequently, the underlying "brakes" on decision-making involve concern about risk. Holding off on making a decision because of "what ifs" only leads to a state of analysis paralysis. Business owners try to find solutions where all variables are controlled, or they simply wait, hoping that with more time another option might materialize. It rarely does. This kind of cautious deliberation delays decisions and actions that help serve customers, gain new business, and improve operations.

You cannot eliminate risk in business. It's an inherent part of the game. There are too many influences, outside factors, and variables to control. You must embrace risk while also trying to reduce or minimize it. It's a balancing act that requires thinking on your feet.

My favorite story about poor decision-making involved company discussions with a former boss about going to an expensive, but critical, trade show event. All of our key partners, vendors, and major clients were set to be there. In April, we submitted a budget to the boss for our participation in the August event. Around the middle of September, a month after the show, he came back to us with his decision, proudly announcing that he was approving the budget for the trade show. He said he'd run the numbers, evaluated the opportunity against the costs repeatedly, looked at the probabilities of signing new business, and had determined it was a good place for us to meet larger prospects. He couldn't figure out our muted reaction, until we showed him the website with photos of the event from the month before.

What he failed to recognize all along was that his decision-making process was broken. His leadership style was like driving a car with one foot constantly on the brake pedal. He was so risk averse that he was constantly working against his own company's momentum.

I recommend setting decision guidelines for yourself and your management team. Here are the basic target timelines:

- Important strategic decisions are given one to two weeks
- Purchase decisions are given forty-eight hours
- Assessments of return on investment, also forty-eight hours
- Operational decisions are given one hour

Situations and opportunities don't all have to be an immediate yes or no. Set reasonable guidelines that allow you to consider options, evaluate your gut reaction, and still make timely decisions to keep momentum rolling.

Sometimes you will be wrong. Sometimes your decisions will clearly be incorrect or misdirected, and you'll need to correct that course to mitigate risk and damage. However, with practice making timely and effective decisions, you'll become good at making course-correcting decisions too, reducing your risk to manageable levels.

Trust yourself and embrace your power to decide. Combine decision-making with active research, reflection, and input from your team. This combination will ensure stronger decisions and a smooth operational momentum to keeping your business momentum flowing.

TIME OFF IS A MUST

———

I talked with a store owner a few years ago who proudly announced that he hadn't taken a vacation in almost five years because he was so committed to his business. I wondered how effective he was without taking time off to recharge his batteries. Was he truly the master of his universe, or was he just a slave of his own making?

Sustaining the long game of being a business owner and building a company places great demands on your mental and physical capacities, as well as your spirit. You need regular downtime to regenerate and sustain your health and well-being.

It's a common problem. Many entrepreneurs feel unable to leave their business operations to others while they're gone. They just don't have enough trust that their team can handle all the details and problems that arise. Sometimes this reluctance is based on real concerns, but more often it's just a story we like to tell ourselves.

The truth is that the only way to know how your business will function without you there, is by leaving. In our advisory work with clients, after they've made good progress in their business operations, we send them on vacation. We make sure that it's a longer vacation than any they've taken before. Of course, they're nervous and scared to leave, but it's an important test of their business systems. Most of the time issues do arise while they are away, and that's the point! The company needs to see where its people, systems, departments, and structure need tweaking and adjustment. It's an acid test that can't be done any other way. The boss comes back, the company reevaluates, and changes are made, until the next vacation test. It's an important part of the rhythm needed to expand and improve your business.

Time off isn't being on a French beach with your smartphone reviewing emails. It's telling your team and clients, "Don't call me unless the business burns down." Wait, that's not right either, because if your business burns down there's nothing you can do to bring it back today, so you might as well keep vacationing.

A compromise solution, if you absolutely can't abandon operations entirely while on vacation, is to set a specific time each day when you'll log in for thirty minutes to address issues, questions, and needs. Make it late in the day and keep it short so it doesn't interfere with your goal of chilling out. Then turn off your laptop and go back to windsurfing. Staff are informed in advance that unless the owner can fix it from Timbuktu, don't bother him. And they don't. You may come back to find there was a major issue, but you couldn't have addressed it anyway, so it's best the team kept you in the dark until you were back. You discover that while you were away, the team managed effectively without you. There were only a few bumps in the road, but they handled those too.

Unfortunately, upon their return many owners make a crucial mistake: they immediately take back the same responsibilities they had before, and once again the business is completely dependent on them.

For example, a client of mine handed off all the quoting, costing, and customer scheduling to his team so he could attend a wedding in New Zealand. Everything ran smoothly while he was away, but when he returned three weeks later, he proudly told me he'd taken all the responsibility back.

"No! Give it all back to them!" I hollered into the phone. "Pretend you didn't come back yet."

He was confused. I explained that by moving those daily

tasks to the team, he could now have time to really focus on growth, strategy, and fishing. He'd taken a major step toward running his business exactly how it should be run. Fortunately, his desire to go fishing more often drove him to immediately inform his staff that they were back on holiday duties. He spent Wednesdays doing planning out of the office, Thursdays working on sales alliances for growth, and Fridays fishing.

So don't return to the same status quo. I am giving you permission right now to put down this book and plan quarterly vacations for the next whole year. I don't mean long weekends, but a week per quarter at minimum. If you don't put it on your calendar with a deposit on a hotel and a plane ticket, it will be too easy to cancel or postpone your deserved breaks.

You know your vacation is long enough when you stop thinking about work. The ideal minimum is ten days. After that you'll be recharged and ready to get home and back to your business—your "baby." I love generating new ideas on the flight home and feeling enthusiastic again about the company I'm building. When you take a solid break, there's an added bonus: you'll get to see the business with fresh eyes again upon returning. That fresh perspective is what's needed to see clearly, think strategically, and generate new ideas for innovation and improvements.

CATCHING UP IS A MYTH

A former client of mine told me that she went to her office over the weekend. Starting Friday night, she worked until 2 a.m. On Saturday she got an early start and worked from 9 a.m. to 10 p.m., then worked on Sunday from 10 a.m. to 3 p.m. She proudly proclaimed that she'd "caught up" on all the tasks she needed to complete.

A week later when I asked her how long her catch-up had lasted, she told me that by Thursday morning she was already behind again. Her catching up had lasted three days, exactly the number of days and nights she'd sacrificed that weekend.

This experiment of hers proved my long-held opinion that there is no such thing as catching up on work. There will always be fresh demands on your time, client and staff needs to attend to, and more tasks than you can fulfill on any given day. For entrepreneurs there's always the next intervention, the next strategy meeting, the next planning session. It's like space travel: first the moon, then Mars, then the edge of the Milky Way, and beyond. Navigating a business is an endless endeavor, so it's never possible to catch up—there will always be something else.

The rate at which you brainstorm new ideas should ideally always exceed what you can implement. You need to selectively focus on where you can have the most impact with improvements and innovations. You're always actively making choices of how to mold and improve your business. By necessity your to-do list will be long. You can't help but look for the next horizon, the next challenge. You should never want to catch up. That would only indicate that you've exhausted your thinking and your company's progress.

By understanding the myth of catching up, you permit yourself to take back control of your time. If you work forty-eight hours a week now, and don't get everything done, then working forty-five hours a week and still not getting everything done would have little change on your business. However, refocusing those three extras hours on strategic initiatives can dramatically impact your company. Refocusing those extra three hours on family or personal time can have a significant impact on your quality of life.

If you plan your workday knowing that you won't get

everything done that crosses your desk, you get to decide what is most important. Don't just dive into a to-do list. Instead, you should carefully select and prioritize, setting the most valuable, realistic goals. At the end of the day you can leave the office feeling accomplished and satisfied.

Overcoming the myth of catching up is something to share with your team. You can help your staff recognize the signs of catch-up behavior. Maybe your managers believe they can get everything done today, and will be caught up by tomorrow. Help them see the drawback of setting impossible expectations, setting themselves up for disappointment and a paradigm of perpetual failure. Help them to see that it can't all be done today, or any day, but by creating priorities, their goals will be more achievable and success more reachable.

I found a viable system for setting achievable daily goals in Brian Scudamore's "Daily Top 3," used by his O2E franchises and his global company 1-800-Got-Junk. Brian and his management teams recognized the shortcomings of trying to catch up on to-do lists that were impossible to get through. They asked all staff, from Brian down to his frontline customer service people, to focus on their Top 3 tasks each day. The concept was to get the most important things done before they became urgent. Staff would choose what they saw as most important to them individually. Signs at the office asked, "What Is Your Top 3 Today?" The entire business would start each day focused on every staff member's Top 3 key tasks.

Cameron Herold, the company's COO, once shared that his Top 3 on a particular day were: 1) completing his marketing budget for the coming year, 2) checking in with his marketing manager on a performance review, and 3) getting concert tickets. When questioned about the concert tickets, he was quick to share that it was an important show for both his wife and himself, so it easily made his Daily Top 3.

This companywide system provides clear focus on critical and strategic tasks that have a big impact. Staff typically achieve their Top 3 and feel a sense of accomplishment and desire to achieve another Top 3 the next day. It accounts for the organization's fast growth and business success.

Get focused on the items that are critical to your success and enjoyment today. Let go of the misdirected belief of catching up today, or ever. Try the Daily Top 3 at your company and let me know the results.

PUT YOURSELF FIRST

———

Are you as tired of the adage, "pay yourself first," as I am? As an entrepreneur, some weeks paying yourself is the last possible option. You use every penny to make rent, payroll, and payable checks to ensure the machine just keeps running. It can feel like a slap in the face when someone throws out that classic line: "Pay yourself first." It's obvious they don't understand the responsibilities that accrue to a business owner—or do they? Maybe there's something to the adage after all. If not "pay" yourself first, maybe it should be "put" yourself first.

Let me demonstrate the principle with some math.

1 = the number of You. You the owner, the one who has taken all the risk, and made all the sacrifice for the business. Maybe you mortgaged your home. You're the one who bears the debt, the stress, and the pressure of the business. You're the one thinking of the business all the

time. You're the source of 90 percent of the ideas and vision for the company. You are the linchpin.

1 to 100 = the number of your Team Members. Each one of them holds a critical role and performs an important function. Often, they know as much about your business operations as you do. Finding them, training them, and keeping them is a process and an ongoing journey. These are people you absolutely care about. You want to see them succeed. You spend more time with these people than most of your family members.

100 to 10,000 = the number of your Customers. You know some of them by name and maybe by their purchases. The majority are names on sales sheets and computer screens. You do everything you can to foster relationships with them, but for most of us, they are primarily transactional relationships. They are all important to our businesses, but we don't really know all of them. For every client we have, there are likely three more potential clients in our marketplace we may have already identified.

So how do I know you need to put *you* first?

If you go away, get sick, or can't be there for the business, the business will fail. With only one of you, it is imperative, critical, and absolute that you lead your company. You can't be replaced with a simple want ad on Indeed.

Wanted: Founder and visionary willing to sacrifice everything.

You've trained your team, found people that fit the company culture and know the business. If any one of them leaves, it's a loss, but it's a loss the company can recover from. It may dramatically impact operations, delivery, and morale, but those impacts will likely be short term. Of course, keeping your people happy and committed is critical. If you only have ten people, every one of them is extremely important to the team dynamic and to keeping things running smoothly. They're not quite as important as you, the owner, but many are pretty close.

If you lose a customer, even if you only have fifty of them active, it's a disruption in operations and growth, but it isn't crippling. Your sales team should have a list of ten more prospects to replace them. For a company with thousands of clients, you're regularly losing clients every month and aren't even aware of it. The average customer is dispensable.

Owner. Team. Customer. That's the order of priority.

When you start out and it's only you, or you and a few employees, everything is ultimately in your hands. Your habit is to do everything, manage everything, and sacrifice every day.

It's time to start breaking that habit. Start a new habit of putting yourself first. It's like a new muscle you need to flex.

Here's how to start:

- Start by leaving early on Fridays, just an hour early, but early.
- When you get a big payment or order, take 1 percent of that cash and move it into your personal account. Immediately go buy yourself something with it. Sure, you'll feel guilty the first few times, but that emotion will pass.
- Start working from home one morning a week.
- Start to book your personal appointments during work hours.

Start to do these things and realize that the business doesn't stop. While you're caring for yourself a little better, the business seems to hum along nicely.

Then flex that muscle with larger actions:

- A salary increase for yourself
- An extra week of vacation
- A new car or other major purchase

Ironically, your team will support you and so will your customers. It's only you who needs convincing.

For a business owner, every day that your business is open is game day. No professional athlete plays their sport every day. Even if they compete one day a week, athletes have a team for support, therapy, and recovery. You, as the business owner, need to recognize that your day in and day out game-day performance requires the same focus on recovery, support, payment, and enjoyment. You deserve it. Seriously, you do, and if you don't make sure you're taken care of, no one else will.

SECRET 97

HEALTH IS WEALTH

—

Many high-profile entrepreneurs and business leaders are fanatics about their health and workout routines. Yet the average entrepreneur can't find the time to get to the gym, go for a walk, or take a yoga class. Meditation? Forget about it.

Why is that? Why is your health not getting any time in your calendar?

The answer is simple: you put the demands of your business, customers, and staff above your own life and health. It's understandable. You've focused on the immediate issues, fires, and daily operations of your company for so long, that it's become your default. You think in the short term about the next order, the next phone call, and the next client request. Your physical health isn't one of your day-to-day concerns. It's much easier to commit to exercising tomorrow, or the next day, if you exercise at all.

Long term, however, you know you can't sacrifice your health and your life for the business. Entrepreneurs all know this when we ask them, but they still don't make decisions based on their long-term health and well-being—until it catches up with them.

I was speaking with a sporting goods store owner who told me that he had a personal heart coach. I wasn't quite sure what he meant, so he explained that he'd been working seventy-hour weeks until he suffered a severe heart attack. His cardiologist assigned him a heart coach to help guide his recovery with exercise and healthy eating. He was instructed not to work more than thirty hours a week, but he confided that he was already back to forty-five or more. To make things worse, he was skipping sessions with his heart coach, and lying to his wife about it.

I told him, "You recognize that no business is worth dying over, right?"

He said, "Yes, but I have all these orders to fulfill, and I have to get to my invoicing."

He didn't understand what was at stake, but I hope you do. No company or entrepreneurial enterprise is worth your life. Most companies have a lifespan of about ten years. Don't let a ten-year work venture steal decades off your life.

Let me share a little secret: you can take time out for yourself simply by scheduling meetings—with yourself. Yes, meetings with you alone. Your staff and customers aren't going to question a meeting you've got in your calendar. Your meeting with yourself might just happen to take place at the gym, or during a walk in the park before lunch. I've had "meetings" with my longtime friend and trainer, Ron, for about ten and a half years now. Best meetings of my week!

Your staff, customers, and other stakeholders in your business aren't concerned about your day-to-day health as their first priority. If you don't stick up for yourself, no one else will.

Your commitment to some form of exercise can be as simple as fifteen minutes with a set of dumbbells in your office or ten minutes of meditation. Schedule that time in your calendar. My calendar has pop-up reminders every day—Walk, Push-ups, Do Squats—just to keep me on track. It's just small eight-minute intervals of my time, but those short "health" breaks make a big impact on my energy, focus, and enthusiasm.

Exercise in any form helps the busy business owner reduce stress and think more clearly. It's necessary to stay fit for the long game of entrepreneurship. A physical care strategy will keep you on the court and off the bench.

It will also be instructive for your team. You need productive, healthy people to help grow your company. A healthy lifestyle should be a priority for everyone in your workplace. People need breaks at work to stretch, walk, or go for a jog, whatever works for them. It helps to decompress and improve morale. So commit right now to make health a priority at your company and watch the energy level rise.

SECRET 98

YOUR ENTOURAGE

—

It's become a cliché in the music business that pop stars travel with a big entourage—a personal chef, a bodyguard, a massage therapist, you name it. While it might seem farfetched, as a business owner you could use an entourage of your own.

Of course, the entourage you need is decidedly different. It's not full time, and it doesn't travel with you. Instead, your entourage should be composed of experts in their field and operate on two levels: professional and personal.

Your professional entourage should include:

- Lawyer
- Accountant
- Business coach or advisor
- Mentors
- Marketing agency or marketing consultant

- Technology advisor
- Senior banker (not just a guy or gal at the branch level)
- Sales coach or sales expert
- Mastermind group

Your personal entourage should include:

- Trainer or workout partner
- Massage therapist
- Chiropractor
- Nutritionist or dietician
- Counselor or therapist
- Clothing consultant or stylist
- Hairstylist or barber

Most often you'll go to them. They are your go-to people in their areas of expertise, and you need to seek them out. It may require some interviews and tryouts to see who's the best fit. They may also change over time, as you recognize what you need, and who fits the bill.

Many will be referred to you by your network. You'll need to test your level of confidence in their skills, and see if it's a good match. Compatibility is an important factor, as well as availability and commitment to your success. I've met some incredible professionals whom I'd love to have added to my entourage, but schedules and other commitments often conflict. Your entourage may change over time with your needs, or as the needs of your business change. Your circle of support will widen, and so will your options.

Before you schedule work tasks and obligations, schedule time with key members of your entourage. Book time with your mentor a month out, so it is in your calendar. Schedule meetings with your accountant months in advance, so they make time for you. If you don't get your entourage scheduled in, you won't be using them to your advantage, and it will affect your personal and organizational performance.

The challenges of entrepreneurship require a business owner to create a network of support and knowledge to lean on and leverage. It isn't about pampering, extravagance, or ego. It's about being a business "athlete" who needs support and training to perform at the highest level, week in and week out. You deserve it, and so does your business.

IT'S A FRIENDLY UNIVERSE

———

Business is a demanding, stressful, and chaotic game of keeps. With all the competition, ups and downs, challenges, demands, and stress of business ownership, it's easy to forget that you are operating in a friendly universe.

If you can strive and persevere through all the losses, heartaches, and setbacks, while keeping your hand on the tiller and your eye on the horizon you'll be successful. Your experience of entrepreneurship will enrich your life and the lives of those you touch—your clients and customers, your staff members and business partners, your family and everyone who relies on your product or service—most of whom you'll never meet.

I initially thought that to succeed in business was simply to outwork the other guy. Then I thought it was just to survive and persist through all the crap long enough that everyone else fell away. I believed it was all about building the ultimate mousetrap of systems and processes to fortify against challenges.

More recently, I've come to appreciate that business is people—striving together, working together to figure out the problems, to innovate and have fun while doing it. Relationships have turned out to be my most valuable key to success. I've learned that a business grows best and most efficiently when everyone grows together.

More and more, I'm interested in collaborative interactions, negotiating over a beer and simply asking what someone wants to pay, finding out who they are and how we can do business together to our mutual benefit. I send cookies, thank you cards, and believe that breaking the "rules" of business is sometimes the best path to success. The longer I've been doing business, the more I feel that there are more secrets to uncover in unconventional processes and creative solutions.

Business is so complex, with so many moving parts, that inevitably you're going to experience crises, operational and systemic breakdowns. Don't confuse that chaos with an unfriendly universe. No great power is working against you, although some days it feels that way. Believe that in fact, the universe is always working to support you and your business. It is aligning opportunities, people, and circumstances to bring you success. It is at work right now supporting you.

The universe may not always appear to be on board with your master plan, but that could mean that your master plan just needs some revision. Be open to the feedback of your team, your customers, your gut, and the marketplace. Together they will lead you and guide you correctly.

Slow down and listen. Embrace the adventure of not knowing, and finding answers among your team, your network, and your customers. Enjoy the ride. Be unconventional. Surround yourself with people who have the talent and commitment to help you succeed. They are emissaries of the universe, and the universe has your back.

CONCLUSION

BECOME A TIGER TAMER

———

To master these 99 Secrets in operating your business is a big task. It can take years to have all these things in place and running smoothly. Please don't judge where you are at now, but simply recognize all the new ideas and approaches you could take to further your success.

Not all of these will apply to your company today. There are seasons and cycles that will make each of these secrets relevant eventually.

I hope you continue to reference this book as a tool to give you ideas and perhaps to remind you of things you lost sight of. Strengthening your skills as a business owner and entrepreneur takes time, focus, and patience with yourself.

This book is the tip of the iceberg. Many of these short secrets are things that we could dive into for an entire week to really drill down on the strategy, mindset, tactics, and implementation. I want to help! I have provided a lot more resources on the website; tools to help, templates to guide you, and a community of people to support you. My mission is to help and empower entrepreneurs. Please visit the website frequently to see what else we've introduced.

www.tigerbythetailbook.com

I recognize that owning a company often feels like having a Tiger by the Tail. It can be daunting and dangerous. I also know that you have the talent, heart, and drive to become a Tiger Tamer. To be that entrepreneur and business owner that others look to as an example of success. To internally know you are in control and creating your dreams.

I believe in you. Go make it happen.

ABOUT THE AUTHOR

———

MARTY PARK is a rare breed. At the age of twenty-one, while most students were neck-deep in homework and weekend plans, Marty was running his first company with eight staff members on payroll. Since then, Marty has owned and operated thirteen companies in industries including software, audio production, food service, franchises, and marketing. Along the way, he's become an expert at business growth and the personal growth that comes with it. Marty is also an award-winning business coach who's worked with clients to conquer adversity, transform their performance, and achieve their ultimate vision of success. In this work, he's been involved in the launch, growth, restructuring, or financing of a multitude of companies internationally.

Made in the USA
Coppell, TX
26 March 2020

17709415R00236